PRAISE FOR
MESSAGE RECEIVED

"Message received indeed! Dr. Mary shares incredible insight into the pitfalls of the message we are sending versus the message that is being received and how critical clear communication is to navigating the multigenerational digital crisis we find ourselves in. Throw in a pandemic twist and her trademark wit, and this becomes a must-read for anyone who wants to break down barriers by better understanding not only themselves but everyone they communicate with."

—JORDAN SHERIDAN, General Manager of Modern
Workplace, Microsoft

"This book is transformative! It has helped me change the way I communicate and how I lead a team of multigenerational leaders and teammates! Mary Donohue is brilliant, and she breaks down each generation, describing what drives their members and their communication barriers! Definitely worth the read!!!!!"

—LESLIE LORENZ, Director of Data and
Analytics, Lululemon

"Dr. Donohue is already an inspiration to so many! In her new book, she expands on her guiding principles to communication. Dr. Mary has transcended the way our leadership team functions in any and every scenario. *Message Received* is a culmination of her organizational experiences plus her unique innovative spirit! Dr. Mary has identified the source and solution to our digital stress. Her subject matter expertise and willingness to forge the path for us all to embrace and thrive in the new digital world makes this a must-read!"

—CHRIS ISHII, President and COO, D4DT, Inc.

"Dr. Donohue has done it again! She has written another must-read for leaders who want to get the most from their teams. Read this book and learn from one of the best leadership minds in the field."

—MICHAEL CAMP, General Manager, Walmart, Inc.

"Dr. Mary Donohue did it again. She created simple yet comprehensive tools to help many generations connect right where they are. This is a must-read and a keeper for your fingertips' resource."

—PAM MCELVANE, CEO of Diversity, MBA Media

"Rarely have I read and reread a book where I have not only highlighted its wisdom but also taken notes. Dr. Donohue's brilliant and pithy tome is sure to become the post-Covid bible guiding the way forward. The charts, which make science simple, are a must. Her talent is further revealed in her ability to make the reader both learn and chuckle at the same time. This is a rarity when many of us are facing our darkest days in this era of disaster. Kudos to Donohue. Get the book now! I hope my friends are not reading this review, because it is going to be your holiday gift."

—NEALE GODFREY, *New York Times* bestselling author, America's expert on family finance

"This book is a must-read!!! It allowed me to understand where teammates were coming from, and furthermore, I was able to take action that paved the path to positive progress in achieving the objectives. More importantly, it allows leadership to be driven with an open mind, as the underpinning taps into one's curiosity and interest. Congratulations, Mary."

—CHRISTINA GARGANIS HOIS, Managing Director Cross Business Risk Capital Markets, BMO Bank of Montreal

MESSAGE RECEIVED

MESSAGE RECEIVED

7 STEPS TO BREAK DOWN COMMUNICATION BARRIERS AT WORK

DR. MARY DONOHUE

Mc
Graw
Hill

NEW YORK   CHICAGO   SAN FRANCISCO   ATHENS   LONDON
MADRID   MEXICO CITY   MILAN   NEW DELHI
SINGAPORE   SYDNEY   TORONTO

1 2 3 4 5 6 7 8 9   LCR   25 24 23 22 21 20

ISBN: 978-1-260-45635-6
MHID: 1-260-45635-8

e-ISBN: 978-1-260-45636-3
e-MHID: 1-260-45636-6

Design by Mauna Eichner and Lee Fukui

Library of Congress Cataloging-in-Publication Data

Names: Donohue, Mary E., author.
Title: Message received : 7 steps to break down communication barriers at
   work / Dr. Mary Donohue.
Description: New York : McGraw Hill, 2020. | Includes bibliographical
   references and index.
Identifiers: LCCN 2020017674 (print) | LCCN 2020017675 (ebook) | ISBN
   9781260456356 (hardback) | ISBN 9781260456363 (ebook)
Subjects: LCSH: Communication in management. | Communication—Psychological
   aspects. | Employee motivation. | Teams in the workplace—Management.
Classification: LCC HD30.3 .D66 2020 (print) | LCC HD30.3 (ebook) | DDC
   658.4/5—dc23
LC record available at https://lccn.loc.gov/2020017674
LC ebook record available at https://lccn.loc.gov/2020017675

Donohue Mentoring System™ is a trademark of Dr. Mary Donohue.

Figure art created by Steven Demelo, Anoo Concept Inc.

McGraw Hill Education books are available at special quantity discounts to use as premiums and sales promotions or for use in corporate training programs. To contact a representative, please visit the Contact Us pages at www.mhprofessional.com.

Dedicated in loving memory of
Bill Donohue and "Uncle" Jim Smith.

And to my family who constantly tells me I am not funny.
I am funny—read the book, you're in it. LOL!

CONTENTS

ACKNOWLEDGMENTS

I have to start by thanking my awesome husband and daughter who put up with me writing on vacations, writing on the walls when I couldn't use a computer, and who valiantly tried to take dictation from my messed-up head to help me get my work done. Thank you for leaving me alone with my research and our dogs to "do my thing." I still haven't gotten over one of you killing Mr. Fish when I was traveling and researching this book, but eventually my grief will subside. Another Mr. Fish would help.

My admiration and respect for my editor Cheryl Segura can't be put into words. We had the idea for this book five years ago, and at our first breakfast together in 2015, we clicked. Then life happened and we almost didn't get the book done. Her tenacity of purpose and her dedication to me are unsurpassed. I also want to thank "Baby" Segura for being so good to Mommy during a very critical time of editing the book. Thanks to everyone at McGraw Hill who was part of Cheryl's team. Special thanks to Nora Hennick, Amanda Muller, Mauna Eichner, and Lee Fukui.

I would not be here without the love and amazing care of Dr. Yasmin Rahim, who works at the Stronach Regional Cancer Centre at Southlake. Yasmin, without you, I think I may have simply asked for chemo all those years ago. With you, I climbed mountains.

A huge thanks to Dr. Hassan Sibai, my brilliant oncologist and his research team, including Nancy Siddiq and Verna Chung, the clinical nurses I have the privilege of working with at UHN. Even though you persist in testing my blood and making me show up for appointments when I really want to forget, I appreciate you. You have not only taught me how to thrive but how to eat and survive. Every visit with Dr. Sibai is a huge intellectual hug. He encourages my research, my routine, and my passion to help others heal.

I would also like to thank Dr. Vikas Gupta, director of the Elizabeth and Tony Comper MPN Program at Princess Margaret Cancer Center, who, along with Dr. Hassan and Dr. Yasmin, encouraged and supported my research pursuits. This wonderful group of doctors and nurses at UHN believe in my research so much they have agreed to run clinical trials on my digital therapeutic, called Footle. A digital therapeutic is an evidence-based therapeutic that is run with software to prevent, manage, or treat a disease, based on the research in this book. Our goal is to help other leukemia and chronic disease patients reduce their stress. Last but not least, I would like to thank Dr. Daria Love, who introduced me to yoga, supplements, and "cleaner" living. Because of all my doctors and nurses, I thrive with this disease, instead of being left to wither on the vine.

Speaking about withering, without my friends, I think I would have just shriveled up and hid. Thank you to Karen Howe for *always* feeding us physically and emotionally. Karen, Randy, Connor, and Maura—you have always been there at critical times in our life and I appreciate it so much. Thanks for introducing my daughter to cooking and all the expensive foods that go with haute cuisine (like caviar—really, Karen?).

Christine Thomlinson and Jane McLeod are both awesome at cooking. My daughter is a fixture at both their houses, usually with her head in their cupboards. (Apparently our house has *no* food in it.) Both are executive working moms and have been my friends since our kids were in daycare together. We have traveled together as families and for girls' weekends. Together, we have drunk too much and eaten some amazing food (and some really bad food tainted by my blood due to my clumsiness in the kitchen). Much to Jane's husband Patrick's chagrin, we have raced to rides at Disney and run to beat the line to meet Mickey Mouse. Heath, Chris's husband, will tell you that, as a group, we have spent far too little time together with Elvis. Last, we have mourned together. We have weathered the storms of parents, parenthood, and pandemics—thank you.

To my dear friend Beth Gordon Henry, who shares three special bonds with me: rescue dogs, martinis, and an occasional really good steak. Your friendship, love, and willingness to teach me "corporate" speak is invaluable.

To the best-selling author Jeremy Miller, my work-husband who is always there for me. He always picks up the phone and always has time for a brainstorm or chat, especially when I just riff on ideas. Keep up the rants, pal; they are awesome.

To Don Loney, my friend and fellow dog lover, who has edited not only my corporate work and helped me with this book but my husband's book as well. We have windsurfed together, enjoyed many a pint or glass of wine together, and really enjoyed our walks with the dogs together.

My thanks to my hero Mike (Michael) Camp, who not only embraced my system at Walmart when we first met in 2012 but championed it. Mike, without you I doubt I would have written this book. Thank you.

Speaking of champions, I couldn't continue without my friend Trish Ronan, who has been my "bestie" since the first day of undergraduate together at the University of Windsor, when people mistook me for her and her for me. Thanks for always taking care of everything and everyone when I needed you, pal. Now please stop spoiling my daughter!

My other champion is Christina Hois, whom my family originally called my "yoga friend" but now calls her "our friend." This giving woman—who is a cancer survivor, warrior mommy, and brilliant banker—is an amazing supporter whose truth seeking in conversation is equaled by her love of Bikram yoga, exercise, and opera. Hopefully we can one day travel to every opera house in the world together!

Whenever I have needed to understand "why," I have called on my pal Jordan Sheridan. He is one of those humans who you meet and immediately like. Thank you, Jordan, for texting, meeting, brainstorming, and always buying me lunch. You are a true gentleman.

Breaking bread with people seems to be a theme so far in this acknowledgment, so why not continue? I have had the privilege of sharing a meal many times with my mentors: Chris Ishii, Mark Tinnerman, Dr. Alan Middleton, Tom Bitove, and John Barnett. Each has unwaveringly believed in me. They have always picked up the phone or bought me lunch. When discussing my ideas and products, at times, they have been harsh and at other times, they have been effusive in their praise. Thank you, boys!

My business coach Samy Chong is not only a brilliant cook and charming dinner companion, he is my philosophical rock who weekly helps me find my way. Thank you, Samy! My dear friend Sarah Collins is my brand coach. Sarah, thank you for encouraging and supporting not only me but my daughter as well. Thank you.

A big thank you to my friend Pam McElvane, whom I met because of my work in Arkansas and who was responsible for me meeting Dr. Ronald Copeland of Kaiser Permanente. Dr. Copeland and Jabo Floyd of Walmart inspired the research that became this book. Pam, thank you for inviting me to present at the Diversity MBA conferences and for always finding me a glass of wine and a sandwich with chips.

Speaking of wine, I have to thank my colleague and friend Mohammad Mahasneh, who, until recently, was director of communications at my company and who continues to be a dear friend.

Mo encourages me and, like me, enjoys a good bottle of Chablis. Mo, thank you for always buying me the best presents, including Veuve Clicquot. Thank you to my friend Marcel Bregstein, the assistant general manager at the Toronto Hunt Club, for his talent as a sommelier and for finding the aforementioned Chablis and champagne. Thank you to my friend Leslie Lorenz Karduck, who had an even worse year than I did but still found time to be my "lifeline" whenever I went to an AI conference (and who, of course, drank wine with me whenever I was in Seattle). Speaking of Seattle, thank you to Dave Heller and Raanah Amjadi, my Envision pals who have become my friends. Thank you both for your support and love and for the drinks!

Last, but not least, I would like to thank my Friday night family, the team at Souvlaki Hut (Queen and Wineva), who feeds me every single Friday night. Because of you, the sadness of always writing alone on the weekends was felt a little less.

YOUR BRAIN: THE GREAT DIGITAL VOICE CRISIS

MY CRISIS—AND YOURS

December 2018 was the start of an awful, rotten, terribly bad period in my life. My dad died suddenly while watching his beloved NBA-champion Toronto Raptors. While I was at his funeral, the government tax auditor called to inform me my company was being audited and I had to meet with their officials the next day. After the funeral and my "visit" with the auditors, I had to go to an appointment with my oncologist. My blood numbers were bad, which meant more time at doctors' offices and perhaps more treatment. To top this all off, four days before Christmas I was rear-ended by a woman who I suspect was texting while driving.

The emergency room doctor diagnosed me with a concussion, a type of brain injury. He advised I might have difficulty communicating and getting things done, which might cause me to become angry and stressed.

He was right.

Over the course of the next year, work was very difficult as I couldn't communicate well. My business suffered, causing me to spiral down into a lethargic depression. I did the minimum, I didn't push myself to try harder, and I didn't do what should have been done. I was ineffective and burned out—I became part of the 67 percent of employees in North America who are burned out at work.[1]

By the time July rolled around, my concussion symptoms were no better, and my oncology team told me they were concerned that my organs were on a "downward slide." My concussion doctors were concerned that I was not showing any improvement. They recommended chemotherapy for my cancerous blood and other drugs for my headaches.

For a few days I sat on my butt, stunned. I didn't tell anyone what was happening because, the thing was, most of my friends were dealing with a lot worse. My depression continued. Suddenly, one day, while sitting on the porch with my dogs and a very strong martini in hand (hey, a girl needs her vices!), I remembered something my darling friend and writing partner Dr. E. Vince Carter once told me: "At your core, you are a universal problem solver. You get shit done. You break through walls using science and common sense." Eric was right—it was time to break a few walls. Work was literally killing me, and I needed to change.

Prior to the start of the COVID-19 crisis and social distancing, in the summer of 2019, I had to social distance to stay healthy and heal. My only connection with people was through a computer. I was no longer flying 30 weeks a year to see clients. I was grounded without a playbook. After all, there are no guidelines for suddenly not having physical contact with people. Digital communication was causing me to fail because I could no longer experience the social cues or body language that would normally guide my comprehension of others' messaging. I occasionally heard a voice on the phone or saw a face on a video call, but I didn't feel the same connection as I would in an in-person meeting or conversation. Emails were misunderstood, text messages were misinterpreted, and social media posts were all misconstrued; this occurred daily. I was exhausted, I became cynical, and my productivity dropped. Social isolation and digital-only communication were causing me to burn out.

I asked my doctors if there was a relationship between the barriers created by digital communication and burnout. Their answer was "we think so," based on research done by the World Health Organization (WHO). In fact, in May 2019, WHO identified burnout, or chronic workplace stress, as an occupational phenomenon,[2] but my doctors didn't have any specific data beyond that. Well, I had data—data I'd been collecting since 2013—and I had case studies that demonstrated the value of clarity in leadership communication. You know, I had always thought of communication as the *cause* of stress, never as a *cure* for stress. So I began to ask the following: Could clarity in digital communication cause a reduction in stress, thereby reducing chronic stress or burnout? Could clarity be the digital "chicken soup" for the soul?

I know now the answer is "yes." If you can figure out what people are trying to tell you, you won't waste time trying to clarify what is being communicated, and this allows you to get more done in less time. If you get more done in less time, the results are having time to yourself, feeling happier and less stressed, and eventually making more money. Like chicken soup, clarity just makes you feel better. By developing a communication wellness program app, I turned around the horrible effects my cancerous blood, concussion, and business were having on me. My oncology team and occupational therapists were so impressed with my sudden progress, they started to conduct clinical trials on the app, helping chronic cancer patients reduce their stress.

Before you say, "This sounds too good to be true" (such as my mentor, John Barnett, told me), understand this is how all good science works. Good science uses replication, solid data, and historical patterns. I use all three in this book. You will read about the history of the science backing the data, data which was obtained over five years, starting in 2014, from over 27,000 people who participated in beta testing, verbally responded to surveys, or took a course I designed and workshops I conducted.

All of this quantitative data resulted in a margin of error of 3 percent, a confidence level of 95 percent, and a response rate of 11 percent, which falls within the average response rate for an external survey, defined as a survey sent to people you don't know. My qualitative data collection began in 2013 and resulted in the coding and analysis of over 5,000 documents. I triangulated this data with a meta study of over 225 academic articles. But it doesn't end there: I also presented my results to other academics for peer review at meetings and conferences throughout the US.

The system I have developed from this data helps you communicate clearly so you can be understood and understand others. Warren Buffett has stated that "if you can increase your ability to clearly communicate you can double your net worth."[3] For the record, I have not doubled my net worth, but that is more than likely because of my shoe addiction!

WE'VE BEEN HERE BEFORE

Because I am a nerd, I know there is a historical link between stress and changes in how we communicate. As an example, let me use the Great Vowel Shift, which began in the mid-fifteenth century and marked the transformation from Middle English to Modern English. Its impact on education, society, and culture was widespread. As the way words were pronounced changed, communication suffered. These changes, just like the move to a digital society with the introduction of the smartphone in 2007, caused a lot of confusion in how people understood each other. This vowel problem lasted for 300 years.[4] Beginning in the mid-fifteenth century, and just like today, the problem lies in our brain: then, as now, people weren't prepared to respond to the communication shift, they had no prior experience, and in the beginning they failed—that is how they learned. That's where we are now failing.

Today, we are in the midst of what I call the Great Digital Crisis, when the message sent is not the message received. My data tells me that we understand only 20 percent of what is communicated through digital technology. We make best guesses the other 80 percent of the time, what I call the **assumption rate**—defined as how often we accept something as certain without proof—which is causing us unheard-of levels of stress.

WHY WE ARE WRONG 80 PERCENT OF THE TIME

Prior to our 24-7 digital workplace, we all had a cognitive superpower at work—we understood each other. We knew when people were angry or disappointed because of how they acted and the tone of their voice. In the 1970s, one group of researchers proved that 80 percent of the time, you don't even need to hear the words being said in a conversation to understand the emotional context of what is going on.[5] Today, the majority of office workers communicate digitally through emails, texts, or virtual meeting programs like Webex. Our cognitive superpowers are restricted by digital interactions, so we are left to guess the meaning of the messages exchanged.

My research proves these guesses are wrong 80 percent of the time because our brains can't identify social cues or patterns of behavior, such as gestures or tone, during digital communication. We are not understanding others, nor are we being understood. When we get things wrong 80 percent of the time, we become exhausted and stressed, and productivity drops. We get ill because our brains can't break through and recognize the social patterns in communication. The brain begins communicating messages of fight or flight, and that is very bad for us, as it leads to acute stress.

WHAT BURNOUT AND FIGHT OR FLIGHT ARE DOING TO YOUR BODY

In a recent study, Gallup found that 23 percent of full-time employees rated themselves as burned out at work "very often or always," while 44 percent reported feeling burned out "sometimes." [6] That adds up to 67 percent of the workforce, which is bad news. That means almost 7 out of 10 people you interact with every day are exhausted, stressed, and not nearly as productive as they could be. And, as if that wasn't bad enough, if you aren't burned out yourself, you have a strong chance of burning out because you are forced to complete the work other members on your team aren't able to.

Dr. Daria Love, a naturopathic doctor and retired chiropractor, notes that personal health costs are the real cost of burnout. Personal health costs associated with burnout include increased use of mood-enhancing drugs, such as Prozac; the onset of type 2 diabetes; gastrointestinal issues; heart disease; high cholesterol; and even death for those *under the age of forty-five*. The workplace cost of burnout is an estimated $125–$190 billion in healthcare spending each year.[7]

The fact that our digital world is so new to our brains means that a team's ability to collaborate is diminished, derailing projects and compromising its ability to solve problems through critical thinking. After thousands of years of using and understanding social cues, our brains are now searching for meaning in **digital social cues**. Digital social cues are patterns in emails, texts, and social media that help people understand the context of the message being communicated. Our brains haven't figured out these patterns yet, meaning we are unable to accurately read social cues in digital messages, including emails, texts, PowerPoint presentations, and virtual meetings. Today's workplace language is rife with roadblocks that our brains can't break through.

The Mayo Clinic has proved that our fight-or-flight response provokes higher levels of adrenaline and cortisol. When applied to language, this means when you find yourself at your desk, unable to understand a message you've received from a colleague, your heart will begin to pump faster, the sugars in your bloodstream will increase, and you will feel a surge of energy. Next, if you don't understand, or if you misunderstand, what the person is saying, you will get anxious because your stress hormones (increased adrenaline) are elevated.

Dr. Daria Love sees the negative physical effects of stress in her clients every day. I asked her why we are experiencing burnout or chronic stress at work, and this was her response:

> In my opinion, there is much more uncertainty in digital communication rather than face-to-face conversation. This uncertainty is created by a lack of filters in digital communication that we have naturally in face-to-face conversation; for example, tone or social cues. Eventually, your brain starts to react to this uncertainty and filters. When your brain filter fails, fight or flight begins.
>
> Fight or flight is an acute response in the moment. If it is constantly happening at work, it starts to affect our perception of events. Fatigue and anxiety begin to weigh you down, affecting your judgments, resulting in less productivity. This creates **chronic anxiousness** at work, defined as an exhausted but wired feeling in the body. Eventually,

chronic anxiousness affects your body, which sets in motion a whole series of events, including, but not limited to, increased heart rate and sweating, or it creates a sense of panic, or it may affect your bowels. Your body can't sustain this stress, so it adapts to it. This is chronic stress or burnout. It can almost be thought of as a protective measure your body is taking to prevent further damage.

In my practice, I have never heard anyone say, "I don't want to work at my job because my work is too hard." What I hear is "my boss isn't clear," "no one is listening to me," or "no matter what I do, I am not heard." If you're not sure where someone is coming from, as humans, our minds begin to build on this, and we add in our own fears and insecurities. Our mind just starts to go off with all kinds of thoughts, keeping your body in a chronic state of stress—burnout.

We have such a volume of information on digital, which in and of itself isn't bad. It's the speed and the digital demands we react to that cause the problem. In a conversation, there is a short time-buffer for your brain when you are talking face to face, as you are assessing tone, body language, et cetera. In digital, the information is overwhelming, and eventually, after being in a constant state of panic, subconsciously your mind just begins to not respond or blank out. Think of this as the "I can't deal with this now" mindset. When this happens, you need to make a quiet space in your day to allow your brain to distill the constant flow of information.

UNDERSTANDING WHY WE NEED QUIET SPACE

To help people begin to see why they need a buffer or some quiet space in their day, I created a simple test. I call it the "How are you?"

test. Imagine I am your manager and we are on good terms. We meet casually in the hall, I ask you the following questions, and you give me the following responses:

Me: "How are you?"

You: "Good."

Me: "How is your day?"

You: "Good."

These are normal responses—no thought required. This is a normal social pattern. People have asked you these questions thousands of times. Your brain, specifically your thinking brain (the part of your brain closest to your eyes), recognizes this. It could see that as your manager, I was not opening up a long conversation but rather following social norms. Now, imagine I sent you the following emails five minutes apart:

Email 1: "How are you?"

Email 2: "How is your day?"

What would you do if you received these two separate emails from a manager?

My research demonstrates that you are unlikely to respond to the first email because you receive 115 emails a day, at minimum, and over 40 percent of them have to be answered. On top of that, you also spend over four hours a day in meetings.[8] That means *seven hours* of your day is consumed by emails and meetings. You're too busy to reply to what seems to be a social query, so you move on to other tasks, but in the deep recess of your thinking brain a message may start to form, causing you to become suspicious: "Wait . . . Why is she asking that? Why does she want to know *how I am*?"

When you receive the second email, that voice gets louder. Again, you hear the message in your head, but now the voice may become guarded. Perhaps you start asking questions like "Does my manager know something I don't?" or "Are people being laid off?" Within seconds, these simple questions have become distracting and put you on edge. Your fight-or-flight response has kicked in.

These same six words caused two very different responses solely because they were delivered in different ways—in person and by email.

But if your brain would have been able to classify my message, recognizing the pattern as it did when we met in the hall, this stress would not have occurred. Your brain is craving classification and social patterns that will enable it to identify social cues in digital messaging. This is the harm of our digital communication, and this is the reason we don't "get" each other digitally. We don't classify social behavior, nor can we recognize the social cues.

DIGITAL SOCIAL CUES

Social cues are patterns of behavior—such as tone, body language, posture, and familiar gestures—that allow us to reduce ambiguity in conversation. Social cues allow our brains to accurately predict the meaning of words and can cause a fight-or-flight response to a trigger. For example, when my brothers and I were growing up, my mother, when she was *really* upset, would yell out every name connected with our household: Mary, Mark, Boson (our dog), Missy (our horse), Billy (our other horse), Louie (our other dog), and Timmy. By the time she got to naming the youngest member of our family, our brother Tim, Mark and I, being the horrible siblings we were, used our cognitive superpowers and made ourselves scarce. Mark and I could accurately predict when we were in trouble based on Mom's tone and her habit of stomping down the stairs. We knew when we needed to take flight and hide from her. We always left Tim as the sacrificial lamb. (Don't worry about Tim, by the way: as the baby of the family, he is so sweet and cute that, to this day, my mom always calms down around him.) Eventually Mark and I would come out of hiding. My fight or flight saved me from more than one punishment.

The same thing happens at work. For example, when I used to start my workdays, if my boss Patrick's office door was closed and locked, I knew it wasn't a great time ask him for anything, for example, a raise. But if I saw Patrick laughing and wandering through the office, I knew it was a perfect time to ask. When social distancing or working digitally, you don't have the advantage of such cues, and you have no idea how receptive the person on the other end of the screen is going to be.

Reframing: Classification

If you read 115 emails a day and only 20 percent of those emails are perfectly clear to you, 92 of those emails are not. You either have to ask for clarification or give your best guess answer, either of which could result in another email back from your equally frustrated team member, and so on.

Naturally, all of this back and forth makes you tired. You begin to feel like you will never get everything done on your to-do list, and you begin to disengage. Once you've disengaged, your productivity falls. At that point, you not only view your work differently, but you are also at higher risk of illness because you most likely skipped the gym to catch up on your work. Eventually, there is no more "me time" to go to the gym or the theater and you exhibit the classic signs of burnout.

In order to avoid burnout, Dr. Albert Einstein sat in a tub and watched the bubbles. His wife guarded this time for him. She wouldn't let anyone talk to him while he was thinking and watching the bubbles. I asked over a thousand people if they could sit in a tub for 20 minutes without their phone; almost everyone I asked under 40 said no. Those between 40 and 60 said, "I think so," and those 60-plus said, "Of course." To reduce your risk of burnout, take a few minutes every day to have quiet. Even three minutes a day will make a difference. Most likely none of us have Einstein-esque ideas, but we all have ideas, and we need to give our brains time to form them.

YOUR BRAIN AND DIGITAL VS. PERSONAL COMMUNICATION

Brains today are under too much unnecessary stress. The average knowledge workers spend 40 hours a week between meetings and writing emails, and then they work overtime to do their "real" work.[9] Fatigue results in a higher assumption rate. As a result of these pressures, your brain lets you down in a couple of ways. First, you cannot think clearly about what others are saying when you need to rush to get stuff done. Second, your brain has failed to adapt to technology.

Your mammalian brain, or midbrain, houses your anchoring moments, or life experiences, that help you frame responses to messages and questions. Your mammalian brain works with your thinking brain to help you comprehend meaning. It's where your brain interprets the data your thinking brain provides. For example, in the "How are you?" test, your thinking brain knew how to respond to face-to-face interaction. Since the spoken questions are so familiar to your brain, it didn't need the mammalian brain to help interpret them.

But when the people in my research group took the test and received the "How are you?" and "How is your day?" emails, their thinking brains didn't recognize them and sent them to their mammalian brains for interpretation. Their mammalian brains then ran through their storehouses of patterns, came back, and said, "I got nothing" (think George Costanza in the TV show *Seinfeld*). These emails created a stressful situation that caused the participants' reptilian brains (the back of our brains closest to our necks and where fight or flight originates) to begin the fight-or-flight response.

Figure 0.1 is a diagram adapted from one developed by St. Michael's Hospital in Toronto. I first became aware of the power of the mammalian brain when I discovered a version of this diagram during a mindfulness workshop.

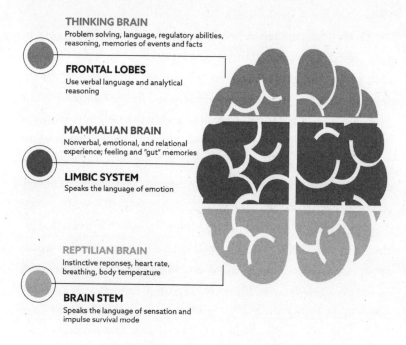

THINKING BRAIN
Problem solving, language, regulatory abilities, reasoning, memories of events and facts

FRONTAL LOBES
Use verbal language and analytical reasoning

MAMMALIAN BRAIN
Nonverbal, emotional, and relational experience; feeling and "gut" memories

LIMBIC SYSTEM
Speaks the language of emotion

REPTILIAN BRAIN
Instinctive reponses, heart rate, breathing, body temperature

BRAIN STEM
Speaks the language of sensation and impulse survival mode

FIGURE 0.1: The Interactive Brain

This is why the message sent isn't always the message received. Digital communication does not afford us the context or social cues that we get from in-person interactions. With the advent of the smartphone in 2007, that normal processing of patterns between our thinking brain (located at the front of our brain) and mammalian brain (located in the middle of our brain) became disrupted to such a degree that we no longer know how to process communication. Our mammalian brain can't find anchoring moments in its library to frame the communication cues we send and receive when we communicate through technology, so it reverts to old communication patterns and applies them, creating digital static.

UNDERSTANDING DIGITAL STATIC

Digital static occurs when people do not have complete clarity in their digital communications, which causes fight or flight. Deb was a happy Luddite when it came to technology. As she tells it, her supervisor didn't care if she didn't understand or use computers. For 25 years she had led in sales revenue and continued to perform at a high level. In 2017, part of the new corporate "productivity plan" was to move her out of the office and have her work from home. The company gave her all the latest technology, and they appointed a new boss who lived in a different city.

One Friday, Deb's new boss, a Millennial, sent her a text that included the word *NOW* in all-capital letters. The new boss, in a rush to get to daycare, didn't mean to capitalize the word, but he felt it was of no consequence. The text was a simple note about a weekly report that was due on Monday, but Deb interpreted that *NOW* as an insult—she had never missed a Monday report. She stressed over it all weekend. By Monday, knowing she could find another senior role in sales elsewhere, she decided to submit her resignation notice to HR by the end of the week.

Early that week, she attended a conference call in which her boss praised her performance in front of the team. She was very confused and asked for a call with her boss, who then explained the error. He apologized for the way he typed the word *NOW* and the unintended stress and anger, which had almost cost the company a high-perform-ing sales rep. This type of cause and effect is called digital static.

Digital static is the gap between what you write in a digital mes-sage and what the person receiving the message understands. For ex-ample, if you are constantly repeating yourself in emails to the same person, you are definitely experiencing static. Digital static is driving the 80 percent assumption rate and 67 percent employee burnout rate. The greater the degree of static, the higher the assumption rate and the lower your productivity and engagement. After all, if you are only understood 20 percent of the time, how can you and your team get work done?

Figure 0.2 demonstrates that the farther we move apart as employees—for example, when we work remotely—the less en-gaged we are with our team because we can't access their social cues. Without social cues, the brain has less to work with in understanding communication. Disengagement is a symptom of burnout, accord-ing to the WHO.[10] According to Gallup, in 2007 the "not engaged" rate was 50 percent;[11] by 2017, ten years after the introduction of the

WHAT HAS CHANGED?

	1990	2000	2010	2020
Offices:	Cubicles	Cubicles	Remote	Hoteling, hot desking
Technology:	Tower or desktop computers	Laptops	Smartphones	Cloud
Work Habits:	9 a.m.–5 p.m.	9 a.m.–5 p.m.	24-7 availability	24-7 availability
Management:	Able to predict how employees and others respond to patterns	Manageable but challenging to predict how employees and others respond to patterns	New patterns arise; disengagement rises dramatically	Disengagement is too high; mammalian brains cannot predict patterns of behavior

FIGURE 0.2: Workspaces and Engagement

smartphone, it rose to an astonishing 85 percent.[12] As shown in the Deb example, the more we rely on technology and increase the time we spend on work without our workmates, the less our mammalian brains can decipher. Figure 0.2 tells the story of this digital impact.

YOU'RE IN FIGHT OR FLIGHT—FIX IT

Constant misunderstanding is like plaque in the brain: it builds up over time. You don't know it's happening until you suddenly realize you are exhausted, disengaged from your job, and angry all the time—classic burnout symptoms.

To limit the negative effects of misunderstanding, identify how your team consumes information or learns through technology. **Learning defaults** are mammalian anchoring cues, including how people work, see, hear, collaborate, and are motivated through learned social cues. They are anchored in patterns learned in school and housed in the mammalian brain. Not knowing your learning default is like trying to tie your shoelaces with one hand—it's really hard to get the job done. You just can't make the right moves. **Digital learning defaults** are the same thing. They are your preferences in how you consume information at work and use your communication skills through technology to get the job done.

As a teacher, I realized that when we can identify with people, we learn faster. They see themselves, or their friends and family, through the "real" examples in the story. To help you contextualize the learning in this book, meet our four "characters" below. They are real folks, but their names have been changed at their request. Please meet Ben the Boomer, Adam the Gen Xer, Trish the Millennial, and Tyler the Gen Zer. A quick review of their ages and their technology preferences are outlined in Figure 0.3.

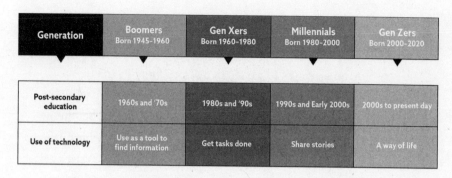

Generation	Boomers Born 1945-1960	Gen Xers Born 1960-1980	Millennials Born 1980-2000	Gen Zers Born 2000-2020
Post-secondary education	1960s and '70s	1980s and '90s	1990s and Early 2000s	2000s to present day
Use of technology	Use as a tool to find information	Get tasks done	Share stories	A way of life

FIGURE 0.3: The Generations and Their Learning Defaults

TWO TYPES OF LEARNING DEFAULTS

There are two types of learning defaults in today's workforce: **share-default learning** and **task-default learning**. In the examples that follow, team members like Trish (a Millennial) and Tyler (a Gen Zer) are part of the share-default learning group, whereas Ben (a Boomer) and Adam (a Gen Xer) are part of the task-default learning group. Each group has different mammalian anchoring cues in response to technology, including how they:

- Work

- See

- Hear

- Collaborate

- Are motivated

Let's dive into each of these cues and how each group responds to them.

Anchoring Cue 1: Working through Technology

Share-Default Group

MILLENNIALS (TRISH) AND GEN ZERS (TYLER)

Team members in a share-default group were trained at school to work collaboratively, usually in groups of four. Teachers, beginning with the great educator Maria Montessori, used group-teaching principles, which caused weaker learners in the group to turn to stronger learners for help. Learning occurs through the *sharing* of information. Anchors for share-default group members, like Trish and Tyler, include, but are not limited to, the habit of working in groups online.

Today, most students use Google Classroom. Group work at universities doesn't require students to be in the same country, and Facebook groups enable students to create learning groups where they can share conversations or projects. All of these group activities enable students to connect with each other even before they start class, whether in grade school or college. Share-default team members prefer to consume technology as a group, through which a number of people contribute. Technology has provided the underpinning for their education and work, and today it drives their belief in the power of superstar teams.

Task-Default Group

BOOMERS (BEN) AND GEN XERS (ADAM)

Team members in a task-default group were trained to work as individuals. At school they sat in single-file rows. Group work wasn't emphasized until, at least, grad school, and rarely was technology, such as conference calling, available to discuss their work. They stayed after school or met at someone's house. For this group, distance education was a lark—it wasn't respected. Anchors for task-default team members like Ben and Adam include, but are not limited to, creating alone and then sharing, and most importantly, the introduction of Microsoft Windows, which enabled them to multitask.

Task-default team members prefer to consume technology as a means to an end—in other words, to get stuff done. Technology has provided the underpinning of their work and driven their belief in the power of superstar leaders like Lee Iacocca and Jack Welch. For these team members, individuals are the winners, even in entertainment (for example, Gordon Gekko in Oliver Stone's satiric movie *Wall Street*).

Anchoring Cue 2: Seeing through Technology

Share-Default Group

MILLENNIALS (TRISH) AND GEN ZERS (TYLER)

The collaborative share-default group shares information through technology. They have done so throughout their entire lives. In school, Trish and Tyler, along with their friends, were trained to find information quickly as a team and then share that information through technology, using, for example, online libraries, YouTube, and Google. As team members, they learned from sharing and working in a group via the cloud. Since they were young, they have been able to connect with anyone anytime through the Internet. Consequently, they prefer to send messages to the group and share information.

This group is fearless when it comes to using technology. To them, new is fun and old is a form of entertainment. They think, "What's the worst that could happen?"

Task-Default Group

BOOMERS (BEN) AND GEN XERS (ADAM)

Working solo, members of the task-default group were trained to find information as individuals, using, for example, card catalogues, library stacks, debate, and discussion. They entered the workforce when computers were plugged into towers to access the Internet.

People like Ben and Adam have taken a long time to come around to trusting the cloud; they trust CDs and memory sticks—you can lock up a disc or a hard drive. Movies and YouTube constantly make fun of this generation for their lack of trust in the cloud.

A perfect example of this is in the movie *Sex Tape*. The movie is about a married couple trying to rekindle their romance who accidentally load their sex video onto the cloud. During a short sequence in the movie, the couple complain about their frustrations with the cloud. Jay, the husband, yells, "Nobody understands the cloud! It's a f***ing mystery!" During research interviews, I have sat with many people who have the same sentiment, but fortunately they didn't mention a sex tape.

This group prefers *tried and true* when it comes to technology. They trust what has worked. They have a strong preference for email, Word, and slide decks. When sending a message to one person or a group, they like to send it in a methodical manner. The technology that helps them do their jobs influences them. Consequently, they prefer to send messages via technology as individuals. They remember that the worst that could happen is losing all their work if Windows shuts down.

Anchoring Cue 3: Hearing through Technology

Share-Default Group

MILLENNIALS (TRISH) AND GEN ZERS (TYLER)
The share-default group uses technology for work, but they are also the first group to use technology for fun and for building relationships. Trish and Tyler organize their lives through online calendars. As Trish said during the interview, "I live and die by my calendar." The share-default group has "Facebook friends" from all over the world, and they chat and have fun together online, including watching YouTube videos and gaming. This group uses technology in all

their experiences—and I mean all. This group is sexting more than any other generation and, according to the research, prefers sexting to the real thing. When they read a message, they want to know how it is going to affect the *experience* of work.

Task-Default Group

BOOMERS (BEN) AND GEN XERS (ADAM)

Time is this group's measurement for success. In my research, almost every time I asked Gen Xers like Adam how they were, they said, "Busy." At a cocktail party, the first thing this group will ask you is "Where do you work?" Next is "How long have you been doing that?" The currency for success in this group is time-on-task. No matter how long they work during a day or week, these group members never feel as if there is enough time. For this group, the home computer and Internet blurred the lines between work and home. For Boomers like Ben and Gen Xers like Adam, work became an obsession, especially with the advent of the BlackBerry phone.

They read a message or listen to a speech in order to understand what they have to do and how this will either add to or lighten their workload. This group still misses the connectivity of the nondigital workplace. They like to meet face-to-face and "hear one another offline." They also prefer the old-fashioned method of sexting—offline.

Anchoring Cue 4: Collaborating through Technology

Collaboration default is defined as how each group prefers to engage in cooperative activities. Collaboration default is your default in how you use technology to get the job done as part of a team.

Share-Default Group

MILLENNIALS (TRISH) AND GEN ZERS (TYLER)

The share-default group prefers to work through *information bursts*. They are instinctual learners and have no problem trying out new things, including new innovations, when it comes to using technology. Calendars are their life, keeping track of their appointments and to-dos. Often, they send calendar invites to participate in a project's to-do. Links are included if further information is required. When someone needs a quick answer from share-default group members, the best route is to text or instant message them. They prefer to collaborate through mobile.

Trish and Tyler like to work wherever and whenever. Their preference is to work on their phone and a laptop or in a group, as they did in school. They believe email can be a problem because they think, "Why communicate with just one person when you can get feedback from everyone?" Collaboration tools like Slack and Microsoft Teams solve this problem: one app, one call, one presentation, and one group of edits. Nothing is too intimate for this group because they have shared their lives online.

Task-Default Group

BOOMERS (BEN) AND GEN XERS (ADAM)

The task-default group prefers *simplicity*. "Get 'er done" is the motto for this group. Don't fuss with the new stuff. Use what works and don't waste their time. Email is used primarily for requesting an action or discussion with team members. Engaging people can still be done on the phone or in person. Calendars are used to create appointments and meetings that organize their lives. For Ben and Adam, collaboration tools—such as Slack, Google Classroom, and Microsoft Teams—are a frustrating secondary or tertiary point of feedback. In my interview with Ben, he stated, "Why do I have to learn something new? I don't have time. Our system works just fine." For the task-default group, PowerPoint is the standard operating procedure (SOP) for any meeting.

This group prefers to collaborate through *solitude*. Give it to them straight and give them time to think. (This group enjoys thinking.)

If you send them messages via email, ensure they contain a logical train of thought with backup. Don't expect an answer right away—this group likes time to think things through. Give them the solitude they need to decide, even if it is just 30 minutes. They will often write down or even draw an answer in their ubiquitous notebooks or on their laptops.

Anchoring Cue 5: Motivating through Technology
Share-Default Group

MILLENNIALS (TRISH) AND GEN ZERS (TYLER)

You can motivate the share-default group with *development*. This group looks for feedback that helps them develop their jobs and tasks. This group struggles to find mentors that will help them do that. Millennials were constantly pushed by their parents into different activities. They always had mentors and coaches and were always given opportunities to learn because, to their parents, they were the most important people on the planet.

The share-default group is also motivated by *conversation*. It's all about time spent with leaders, and the conversations they have with them are a reward. They appreciate when leaders send them short texts or emails on a job well done. But they really appreciate receiving praise in a group chat or on a collaborative platform. Money has never been a motivator for this group. Rather, experiences and "dreams"—including dream vacations, dream lives, and dream jobs—motivate them. They have the benefit of parents who are obsessed with them, which is a lovely privilege that was unheard of before their generation.

Task-Default Group

BOOMERS (BEN) AND GEN X (ADAM)

You can motivate the task-default group with *money*. At work, they know bonuses are given for tasks, not how many "team members" the company develops. This was the tradition when Boomers adapted to the digital workplace in the 1980s, and the tradition hasn't changed with Gen X. This group's default is to work hard and fast, and they love every minute of it.

The task-default group is also motivated by *priorities*. Both Boomers and Gen Xers are constantly on their phones. Some even race to see how fast they can answer an email from their boss. This group has become famous for not taking enough vacation time. They have always had to work. Because they had children later in life than previous generations, they are the first generations that have had to manage their parents as they've grown old and, at the same time, get their children through high school. Align work and purpose with their priorities, and they will work hard.

➤

Figure 0.4 introduces the term **digital emotional intelligence (DEQ)**, which determines if you are task dominant or share dominant. In Chapter 4, we explore DEQ further, but right now it is important to appreciate that DEQ is your ability to recognize patterns in the messages you receive, enabling you to understand what people are saying to you and predict how people are going to engage with you. It empowers you to solve problems quickly and effectively. The following chapters are a guide to cultivating your DEQ.

The visual in Figure 0.4 enables you to see the difference between the default groups while also enabling your brain to clearly see the difference in default patterns. For visual learners, you can copy and print out the figure, then refer back to it when you need to.

	Share-Default Millennials and Gen Zers	Task-Default Boomers and Gen Xers
DEQ Anchoring Moment		
Learning Habits	7 minutes	22 minutes
Learning Tools	Together	Solitary
Leadership Learning	Democratic	Autocratic
Compensation	Experiences	Money
Performance Appraisals	Daily	360°
Technology Preferences	Shared	Private
DEQ Default Response		
Calendar	My rule	My role
New Technology	Demand	Dismiss (no time)
Email	Secondary	Primary
PowerPoint	Optional	SOP (standard operating procedure)
Instant Messaging Yammer, Chat, Text	Constant	Intimate

FIGURE 0.4: Digital Emotional Intelligence

Table 0.1 is designed to enable you to provide the environment for communication that enhances problem solving by presenting each default group with the correct stimulus. It can be used as an *at-a-glance* aid to help you understand and avoid common workplace misunderstandings that often fester and cause chronic stress and burnout.

TABLE 0.1: **Common Problems and Their Solutions**

Problem	Share-Default Millennials and Gen Zers	Task-Default Boomers and Gen Xers
Reduced problem-solving activities	Create online experiences that enable this group to develop a solution together	Give the team a virtual whiteboard and ask them to "draw" the problem
Hasty and inaccurate messages	Use sentence patterning that outlines the experience and what is required	Use sentence patterning that explains timelines and the roles of the team members
Disengagement	Use a collaborative technology such as Slack or Microsoft Teams	Demonstrate simplicity and the time-saving value of collaborative technology
Lack of traction and follow-through	Motivate with development activities or time off	Motivate with money

As we learned in this chapter, it is important to understand how your brain struggles with digital technology and how it has been trained to "see" work through technology. Members of the task-default group and the share-default group "see" or learn from technology differently, meaning they consume communication differently. Understanding how they consume technology can help you begin to categorize how others on your team "see" work.

Once you begin to place team members like Ben, Adam, Trish, and Tyler into communication categories, you will begin to notice the differences in how the four different generations learn through technology. This will enable your mammalian brain to start identifying and classifying the behavior you see, enabling you to be right

30 percent of the time rather than 20 percent of the time, as occurs when you "listen" digitally.

In the first chapter, I give you a couple of new "plays," to use a sports analogy, to help you create a mental playbook that will enable you to lower your stress through categorization.

TOOLS IN THIS BOOK

Throughout this book I will reference the different generations quite often. In order to avoid repetition of the years in which each generation was born, you can flip to Table 0.2 for reference at any time.

TABLE 0.2: Generation Designations

Categorization	Birth Years
Boomers	1945–1960
Gen Xers	1960–1975
Millennials	1980–1995
Gen Zers	2000–2020

You will also find figures and tables throughout the book that you can copy, print out, and place on your desk, or take pictures of them, for your reference. These visual learning tools explain terms and social cues and will help trigger your brain to identify patterns in digital communication.

I've also included a list of terms in the Glossary, found in the back of the book, that you may want to revisit at a later time. Each time you see a word in bold in the text, you will know you can find that term in the Glossary.

CHAPTER ONE

STEP 1:
STOP ASSUMING

UNDERSTANDING EACH GENERATION'S COMMUNICATION STYLES

Working digitally causes us to misunderstand, or assume we understand, someone's digital message to us 80 percent of the time. So if we work 253 days of the year (not including vacation), we are frustrated and tired for about 202 days a year. But by learning how to classify people we communicate with into groups and identify patterns of behavior common to each group, we can transform our workdays—and our stress levels.

Generations are defined by many things. In my case, I define them by their familiarity with technology and the educational teaching trends of the time:

- Boomers (born 1945–1960), Gen Xers (born 1960–1980), Millennials (born 1980–2000), and Gen Zers (born 2000–2020). The next generation, the Alphas, began being born in 2020.

- According to Pew Research Center and Gallup, today's workforce is composed of approximately 11 percent Boomers, 43 percent Gen Xers, 44 percent Millennials, and 2 percent Gen Zers. My research demonstrates the largest gap in miscommunication exists between Gen Xers and Millennials. Gen Xers process technology through the lens of task and time, while Millennials process technology through the lens of sharing and development. These different language processing behaviors produce an ineffective communication exchange that, if not stopped, causes chronic stress and lost income.

- Companies risk $135 million for every $1 billion spent on a project, and new research indicates that $75 million of that $135 million (56 percent) is put at risk by ineffective communications.[1] Since ineffective communication leads to disengaged employees, these findings indicate a critical need for organizations to address communications deficiencies at the enterprise level.

Throughout the book I introduce new terms and definitions for clear communication (as mentioned, the Glossary in the back of the book provides definitions for these terms). Throughout the chapters you will see visuals designed to provide visual cues to help you retain your learning.

CATEGORIZATION:
THE BRAIN'S SHORTCUT

One of the great abilities of the brain is categorization. Categorization gives the brain a shortcut that enables it to clarify a message or situation. For example, through trial and error, the brain evolved to categorize the difference between going after prey and being preyed upon.

Today, your brain's challenge is not to "distinguish prey and aggressors from other kinds of objects," as psychologist and categorization expert Alfonso Caramazza explains,[2] but rather to categorize patterns it sees in the messages you send and receive. According to *Business Insider*, the average person picks up or looks at his or her phone over 2,600 times a day.[3] Compound that with the four hours a day you spend in meetings and the minimum 115 emails you receive a day, 40 percent of which have to be answered—it's no wonder why you, like me, have a sore head.

In my research for this book, no matter who I talked to—physicians, knowledge workers, or executives—almost 7 out of 10 people told me that they were suffering from one or more of the following symptoms: exhaustion, increased mental distance from one's job (disengagement), and reduced professional efficiency (low productivity). Strangely, or maybe not so strangely, these are also symptoms of a concussion. I then asked CEOs of companies, both large and small, if any of this made sense or was somehow showing up in their workforces. What they told me was startling. The number one medical expense being claimed on benefits is mood-enhancing drugs, such as amphetamines, Valium, and meds for ADHD. All of this aligns with Gallup's research on burnout.[4]

I don't think everyone has a concussion, but the root cause of our stress and anxiety is that the brain, as smart as it is, has not adjusted to technology. Technology is the barrier to understanding, and this hurt is expressing itself in the symptoms of disengagement, fatigue, confusion, drowsiness, and low productivity (again, symptoms of both concussions and burnout). So how can we help our brains solve this problem? Let's start by looking at why the problem exists.

THE DIGITAL BARRIER

When you read a text or an email from your colleagues, you hear your own voice in your head as it attempts to decipher the meaning of what you're reading. Unlike being face-to-face with your colleagues, you don't hear the tone in their voices, and you can't see their facial expressions or body language. In other words, you are listening to *you* trying to be *them*. I call this the "voice in your head syndrome," and it is like a bad *Saturday Night Live* sketch, as this personal example of *not* hearing someone's digital communication demonstrates:

> I texted my husband to tell him my flight was landing on time and that I was glad he was picking me up because it was pouring rain. He texted me back and said, "I can't pick you up. There is a playoff hockey game tonight, traffic will be horrible downtown, take a cab home." I texted him back, "REALLY???"
>
> What he *heard* was my surprise that there was an important playoff game. What I *meant* was I was shocked he was not coming to pick me up after a long business trip. I was trying to convey "Are you kidding me? Trying to get a cab at this time of night in the rain is going to be impossible, and I will be soaked."
>
> In this situation, my husband and I didn't hear each other, and as a result, when I got home—soaking wet, barefoot, and holding my shoes and new purse under my coat—I made sure we both understood what "REALLY???" meant for future reference.

As funny as this story may seem *now*, this domestic misunderstanding was caused by the fact that my husband didn't *hear* the tone of my voice; he didn't *see* my body language; and I didn't *see* his weary face and body language that said he couldn't stand any more time on the road after a long day. This lack of human context caused both of us to miss the subtle cues associated with a conversation.

Those subtle cues are what we call nonverbal communication. In his 1971 book *Silent Messages*, Dr. Albert Mehrabian demonstrated the importance of nonverbal communication. He concluded that trust in messaging is based 55 percent on a speaker's body language, 38 percent on the "musicality" of the speaker's voice, and only 7 percent on an assessment of the credibility of the message itself. Today, because we communicate digitally, we miss these critical nonverbal communication cues.

WHAT ARE THE DIGITAL *VERBAL* CUES WE ARE MISSING?

When you were growing up, you knew the difference between "right now" and "*right now*" by an adult's tone of voice or physical actions. When my mom really didn't care if we got something done, she would say, "Just do it right now, please." When she really wanted it done, she would say, in a much louder tone and with a wooden spoon in hand, "*Just do it right now.*" Her voice expressed an unmistakable social cue.

One of the students in my beta group used the following example to show how a lack of social cues has impacted his job:

> When I first started to work in the nineties, I knew my boss was angry when he stormed across the room. I figured it wasn't a good time for me to ask for Friday off. However, today I have no idea what mood my boss is in when he receives my emailed request for the day off. Neither do I know how people are reacting to what I write in my emails

or what I say in a virtual meeting without video, which is ba-
sically all the time because everyone my age hates video.
I just don't know!

For most of your life, the way you have come to understand another person—be it a teacher, boss, or coworker—has been based
on your mammalian brain's response to how that person sounded or
the look on his or her face. As my "How are you?" test example in the
Introduction demonstrates, we cannot read those cues in the technology we use to communicate.

So where does that leave us? How do we solve this problem? The
answer lies in learning patterns in digital communication. We can
get started by understanding generational anchoring benchmarks
(GABs).

UNDERSTANDING GABS

Generational anchoring benchmarks are cues that help you understand and categorize messages. Each of the GABs reflects how the
economy, technology, leadership trends, and teaching trends have
impacted each generation and how these impacts affect each generation's use of technology at work.

Here is how GABs work:

1. GABs help your brain fill in missing information it needs
   to enable it to categorize the message you are sending
   or receiving. GABs categorize by generation, and these
   generations are Boomers (born 1945–1960), Gen Xers
   (born 1960–1980), Millennials (born 1980–2000), and
   Gen Zers (born 2000–2020), along with Cuspers, (people
   who were born plus or minus five years of the start or end

of the birth years of each generation). See Table 1.1 for reference.

2. Categorization enables you to see patterns in messages.

3. Once your brain learns these categories, it identifies the patterns associated with each one. For example, Millennials tend to be less formal than Boomers. Once you learn to categorize, the social cues or patterns characterized by GABs will help you understand how to best connect with a person or team or how to motivate others by using the right words, technology, and meeting structures.

TABLE 1.1: **Generational Cuspers**

Categorization	Birth Years
Boomers	1945–1960
Cuspers: Boomers/Gen Xers	1955–1960
Gen Xers	1960–1975
Cuspers: Gen Xers/Millennials	1975–1980
Millennials	1980–1995
Cuspers: Millennials/Gen Zers	1995–2000
Gen Zers	2000–2020

WHERE'S WALDO? FINDING PATTERNS

GABs are the key to understanding the words, sentence patterning, and social cues that stimulate your audience's subconscious. They enable you to increase your rate of accuracy of understanding by 10 percent.

Social media is like *Where's Waldo,* in which you have to find the pattern of Waldo's hat and other attire: it introduces you to lots of interesting, colorful people that you can get lost looking at, but to solve your communication problem you have to be able to "see Waldo," and like Waldo, every generation tends to wear pretty much the same outfit. To reduce assumption, you need to recognize these patterns.

In order to understand some generational trends and how they can help you communicate most effectively, I present the following real profiles of Ben (a Boomer), Adam (a Gen Xer), Trish (a Millennial), and Tyler (a Gen Zer). I have highlighted the patterns' cues for you. Based on my research and experiences with teams, I have found that 5 percent of the North American population doesn't fit the standard generational behavior patterns.

MEET BEN THE BOOMER

Ben is a Baby Boomer (also referred to as a Boomer). He started elementary school in 1957. He falls into the task-default group. Ben wants just the facts, he is clear and succinct, and his messages are clearly written. He also doesn't share anything personal, and he just lists his work highlights on social media. This suggests that Ben's digital tone of voice is formal.

Categorization: Boomer, Born 1945–1960

Ben went to university in the '70s. His first full-time job came soon after he graduated from university, and over time his career has advanced. These clues allow us to categorize him not for age discrimination but for communication clarity. I have heard from a few Boomers that they don't list their age or the dates they attended school on their profile pages because they feel they will be discriminated against. However, even if these dates are absent, their communication patterns will indicate that they are Boomers.

Generational Anchoring Benchmark: Formality

Ben's pattern of language and his depiction of his accomplishments show us he likes to build. *Building* is a Baby Boomer's primary listening anchor. Boomers, like Ben, converse in person or digitally to build, which means they want to hear how a project is progressing, know if there are any problems, and understand what to do to solve them. Boomers have built bureaucracies, companies, and amazing volunteer structures.

Boomers used their influence to shape the past millennium and along the way created some wonderful structures for the generations that have followed. They have been driven throughout their lives to combat impermanence. Why? In their youth, they lived under the constant threat of war and the nuclear bomb; in fact, they had to learn to hide under their desks to protect themselves from those threats. Boomers grew up knowing that everything could be lost in a minute or their little corner of the world might end at any time, which was reinforced by the assassination of President Kennedy. This led their mammalian brains to combat impermanence with permanence and build a legacy.

Boomers like Ben build teams and cultures. Speaking from experience, people like Ben are wonderful people to sound out if you have new ideas. They have a rich history of problem solving. Pairing a Baby Boomer with a Millennial or Gen Zer will create a wonderful work parent-child relationship for building culture through conversation, even if it is virtual. My experience with the Bens of the world is that they love technology because it allows them to converse with more people and stay in touch with everyone. Perhaps that's why they like Facebook so much.

Listening Behavior Patterns: Well Written

Cues: Ben appreciates a formal, detached style of writing.

Patterns: Ben's use of language demonstrates his anchoring benchmark. Ben, like most of his generation, is a builder.

Listening Cues: Auditory Words

Baby Boomers listen to or process information in an auditory capacity. They don't use numbers, pictures, graphs, or videos—they just use words. In their youth, boomers learned through auditory channels. For example, if I ask Ben, or any Boomer, about JFK's assassination, each of them will have a clear recollection about where they *heard* the news: on the radio. For Boomers, radio was their primary source of information and television slowly became their second. This generation was also required by their parents and teachers—who had just come out of two world wars—to be on top of world events. As children, Boomers read the paper and reported on what they read. Conversations around the dining room table and in the classroom required focus, and Baby Boomers had to speak their part.

Email and Social Media Patterns: Letters

Digital mirroring is the practice of giving information to people in the same manner they provide it to you and others. Boomers were introduced to technology through phones and then television, and they prefer to use technology in a formal and respectful manner. Therefore, to be successful with Boomers, you should share information with them in a more formal method than you would with a colleague who has only been in the workforce for a few years.

When you receive a text or an email from a Boomer, it is typically longer than texts or emails from younger generations. Boomers' generational anchoring in building drives them to provide detail and context. In an email from a Boomer, look for patterns that include correct grammar, clear instructions, and important details. To mirror this, write your emails to them in a more formal manner, which will help their brains make sense of the messages you are sending. Here are some examples of effective and ineffective writing tips to communicate with Boomers:

- **Salutation:** "Dear Ben" or "Hello Ben." Don't start with "Hey Ben."

- **Subject line:** Be clear and succinct. Use words, not symbols (like a smiley face).

- **Body of email:** Ben has an auditory task-dominant brain. Therefore, you should write full sentences that describe plainly the who, what, when, where, and why, if necessary, of your request or message.

- **Sign-off:** Should be formal. For example, use "Sincerely" or "Regards."

By following the structure above, you will have provided Ben the Boomer with a pattern his brain is familiar with—a letter. When Ben began his first job, he used an IBM Selectric typewriter, envelopes, and stamps. Colleagues sent formal memos around the office. He communicated with his family via letters because long-distance telephone calls were still very expensive. When Ben sees your email, his brain will immediately recognize this pattern, and he is more likely to respond to this pattern than when his brain sees a pattern of short, casual bullet points.

As Mr. Buffett pointed out, to build your network you must communicate clearly, and emailing based on the digital listening preferences of Boomers, which revolve around building, will help you do that.

How a Boomer Listens: Spitballing

To problem solve or brainstorm ideas with a Boomer like Ben, you must talk things through on the phone or in person. Just ask them for ideas based on their experience about how you can solve a problem or accomplish what you have to get done. My friend Don calls it spitballing, where you just chitchat and see what comes up. It's how we humans solved problems before Google. We asked others for their opinions and advice instead of asking a search engine.

For example, when my uncle Jim worked at Merrill Lynch years ago, teams would end the day by reviewing problems that occurred over the last 24 hours and discussing problems that might arise the next day. Problems would be assigned a level of importance, and managers would think about a solution or a policy that could help them solve those problems. The managers would meet the next morning and present a resolution that would then be voted on. The managers talked with one another. They didn't email. This is why Baby Boomers begin to feel disengaged when they don't have an opportunity to discuss problems. They like to talk through situations, and they are good at doing so. They quite naturally create logical sequences out of engaging conversations.

Words and Phrases to Ensure You Are Heard

- Words and phrases that work best are "hear," "listen," "one to one," "tell me," and "I hear what you say."

- Other phrases to use to engage Boomers include "What is your opinion?" and "based on your experience . . ."

Digital Listening Stressors

- To improve your clarity, avoid stressors such as "not having the opportunity to discuss matters and talk them through" or "not being listened to."

MEET ADAM THE GEN XER

Adam went to school in the '70s and '80s. He has never been a slacker, but he's also never been a dreamer. He is a doer. Gen Xers have always been underestimated and cynical; *Time* magazine wrote them off in 1990 as a generation of slackers. Perhaps this spurred them to be just the opposite.

Categorization: Gen Xer, Born 1960–1980

Adam, like most Gen Xers, has jumped jobs. This is because of recessions—very few Gen Xers have been able to stay in their careers for more than 20 years. Gen Xers are less formal than Boomers but far more results focused. This has enabled Gen Xers to embrace a more casual approach to work—for example, no ties or suits—but also embrace a strong focus on looking professional and working until the job is accomplished.

Generational Anchoring Benchmark: Get It Done

Gen Xers get the job done. They are tenacious, and this tenacity of purpose enables them to get back up after failures, of which they have had many. They don't let failures get them down, and instead, they turn them into positives. They know how to do more with less, but they expect others to have the same ability.

They focus on the main task, and they are great strategists. They want details about how a project is moving along and what problems need to be solved. Gen Xers are steadfast and respond well to both being assigned work and assigning tasks. They will put their heads down to get the work done. They encourage others but are baffled by people who aren't self-starters. They have no patience for team members who need affirmation and attention every step of the way. When constantly asked for direction on a project, a typical Gen Xer would think, "Why can't you just get the job done? Figure it out on your own and then bring it to me."

Gen Xers are the smallest of the cohorts, and this has made them real scrappers. They have always had to hustle for what they need, since no one really "hears" them. They are sandwiched between two larger cohorts, Baby Boomers and Millennials. Gen Xers are the first generation ever to graduate from college during a recession and the first generation to have a 12 percent interest rate on their student loans. When they graduated, they became "jobbers" who did a little of this and a little of that. They hustled to get work and are now driven by the need to earn money—their favorite reward. Gen Xers are excellent mentors for Gen Zers, as they both have very strong work ethics.

Listening Behavior Patterns: Goal Based

Cues: Gen Xers appreciate a "goal" style of writing.

Patterns: Gen Xers have a commitment to strategic and operational excellence. If you want Adam to pay attention to you, engage him through the project's ROI or how much money will be made or lost if decision X is made.

Listening Cues: Visual

Gen Xers listen to, or process, information in a *visual capacity*. Gen Xers were brought up with TV dinners and TV tables. It all began with Walt Disney's TV shows. Many Gen Xers can remember sitting with their parents, eating dinner, and waiting for Mr. Disney to introduce the shows on Sunday nights. Later in their lives, Gen Xers would gather together to watch their favorite shows—for example, *Cheers, Family Ties, Friends*—and this resulted in water cooler conversations. This generation made a bigger deal about the Super Bowl commercials and halftime shows than the actual games.

Email and Social Media Patterns: The To-Do List

To digitally mirror Gen Xers, look at the language they tend to use and their methodology for writing emails. They tend to read quickly, so ensure your email is 250 words or less, which takes under 10 seconds to read. Make sure the email looks like a to-do list. Draft the email in bullet point form and ensure you have attached documents, if necessary, not just links.

Take clues from the emails you receive from Gen Xers. When you receive an email from a Gen Xer, you will see that it includes bullet points and short paragraphs, and it often gets straight to the point. There is the occasional spelling error, but that is not because they don't care; it's because no one who has ever had a BlackBerry has ever become accustomed to the keyboard on today's smartphones! When sending an email, don't use "Dear X." Instead, say, "Hi," unless the culture you are working in requires something more formal. An effective email to a Gen Xer would look like this:

Salutation: "Hi Adam"

Subject line: Concisely listed problem

Body text:

Background

- Bullet point one

- Bullet point two

What Has Been Done to Date?

- Bullet point one

- Bullet point two

<u>Next Steps</u>

- Bullet point one

- Bullet point two

Sign off: "Thank you, M" (your initial)

Notice the lack of formality—just get right to the point and you will get their attention.

How a Gen Xer Listens:
Whiteboarding and Notebooks

Gen Xers are visual. Walk into a Gen Xer's office and you will see a whiteboard. At meetings, Gen Xers always have a notebook with them. They *love* their whiteboards and notebooks. In fact, they began the process of whiteboarding in a boardroom. They love drawing answers to problems, and they brainstorm visually.

Gen Xers communicate through PowerPoint. If Millennials and Gen Zers feel their Gen Xer bosses are failing to understand their proposals, I recommend that they draft a PowerPoint deck to help their Gen Xer bosses see the problem, the solution, and their ramifications.

To start a conversation with a Gen Xer, ask them *how busy* they are at work, not if they are busy. You know they are busy, so give them a chance to make their response a little more detailed.

Words and Phrases to Ensure You Are Heard

- Words that work best are "see," "focus," "outlook," "diagram," and "snapshot."

- Phrases to use to engage Gen Xers include "What is our strategy and tactic?" "help me picture . . . ," and "What is your perspective?"

Digital Listening Stressors

- To improve your clarity, avoid stressors such as "no, you won't." Gen Xers are quietly resilient. When you say, "No," they say, "Oh yes, I will."

MEET TRISH THE MILLENNIAL

Trish is a member of the Millennial generation, one of the most maligned and misunderstood generations of all time. Millennials like Trish came of age in a period of economic development. As children, their parents kept them busy with scheduled days and very little down time. Their parents supported, and continue to support, them through every success and hurdle. Trish is fun, engaging, and definitely informal. She takes advantage of social media by incorporating it when she engages with people.

Categorization: Millennial, Born 1980–2000

Trish, like all Millennials, had the opportunity to go online in grade school, using technology in order to share homework and life stories. Trish has a share-dominant brain. She *shares* her success with others.

Generational Anchoring Benchmark: Adapt, Adopt, Improve

Millennials have been exposed to change and dramatic shifts in policy. They have been forced to adapt to circumstances their entire life, primarily because they've seen institutions like marriage, organized religion, banking, and government fail in a spectacular fashion. They are the first generation to experience multidivorces, and they are also the first generation to come home to empty houses. But, with their parents' help and very structured lives at home and at school, they learned to excel at adapting within structures. Millennials always adapt, adopt, and improve. They thrive on change and success. When your team needs to innovate, this is the go-to group. As they grew up, they were driven by the need to be liked, with Mark Zuckerberg's Facebook shaping their world. They are the first generation to have a history online that anyone can check out.

Millennials are the first generation to adapt technology as a tool for friendship and news. Millennials were trained to get an *A* in school, and Millennials' parents were the first people ever to put stickers on their car that said, "My child is an honor student." This led to a number of consequences and was compounded by the need to showcase a great profile on social media later in life.

Millennials are the first generation to have become obsessed with marks in school. This gave rise to the helicopter parent, who was always around, always helping, always encouraging, and always prodding teachers, including university professors and deans, to rethink their child's projects' markings. In some cases, teachers became students' adversaries instead of their advisors and educators. These relationships shaped Millennials not only in how they view authority but in how they view messages and assignments from authority.

Facebook literally changed their lives because it suddenly allowed them to be able to share their ideas, lives, loves, and hates online. This group learned to share with others in brief updates, pictures, and likes and dislikes.

Listening Behavior Patterns: Sticky Notes

Cues: Millennials appreciate quick and casual messages.

Patterns: Millennials, with working parents and stepparents, lived in very busy households. In premobile phone days, they became accustomed to communicating with their family by writing on sticky notes and pasting them to the fridge. The lives of these latchkey kids were dictated by a calendar that was stuck to the fridge, with short, quick notes about their activities. Therefore, when a Millennial communicates, it is in a staccato style. Give them information bursts that can fit on sticky notes.

Listening Cues: Kinesthetic and Action Based

Millennials process information kinesthetically, meaning they actively listen and communicate. Trish not only shares her success, but as a Millennial, she is very clever in how she shares and engages. Millennials are the most genial of all the generations online, and in my research, I found that Millennials were the most authentic online and rarely held back anything.

Email and Social Media Patterns: Short Message System

When Millennials first started communicating, they ran into technology restrictions, such as tweets that were limited to 140 characters and limited texting capabilities that made writing out long words frustrating. So they began to invent and use short-form words and phrases, and a casual short message system became their norm. When you receive an email from a Millennial, it will be casual and to the point, often accompanied by a link that explains more. When you want to engage Millennials through email, think about the casual, short message system they use. For example:

Salutation: "Hey Trish"

Subject line: The action required or problem that needs to be solved, such as "Survey status—need by 3 p.m. tomorrow"

Body text:

- First line: "What is the status of survey that is going out November 1? Is it ready? Are all the edits included? Do you foresee any problems?"

- Second line: "Please provide me with an update by 3 p.m. tomorrow."

Sign-off: "Thanks, M" (your initial)

After sending the message, send a calendar invite for the survey due at 3 p.m. to reinforce the action required. Remember, Millennials' lives were ruled by a calendar when they were younger.

How a Millennial Listens: Teaming

Use technology to problem solve and brainstorm with Millennials. They always enjoy seeing each other in person, but it's not necessary to connecting. They can use Google Hangouts, Microsoft Teams, Slack, and Facebook groups to brainstorm and solve a problem. But remember to give them the problem and the deadline and then allow them to use the technology that enables them to flourish.

Words and Phrases to Ensure You Are Heard

- Words that work best include "socialize," "pull some strings," and "make contact."

- Phrases to use to engage Millennials include "What do you think?" and "How can we adapt or improve this?"

Digital Listening Stressors

- To improve your clarity, avoid stressors such as "this is your fault" or "you are not good enough." Millennials are the generation whose parents told them they were the "best" and that everyone was always a winner.

MEET TYLER THE GEN ZER

Tyler recently graduated from college and is brand new to the work-force. Tyler grew up with and in technology, and you could say that he is "curating his own image." He is very conscious of his visual image and his share-dominant brain.

Categorization: Gen Zer, Born 2000–2020

Tyler graduated in 2018 and was a keen volunteer at school. He expects you to interact with him. Sadly, the obsession with academic grades continues with his generation. I say "sadly" because, speaking as a recovering academic, grades aren't as important as learning *how* and *why* in college. It's never about the grades; rather, it's about *how to think*, not how to get an *A*. (But my Gen X bias is showing.)

Generational Anchoring Benchmark: Interactive

Gen Z is the first interactive generation, meaning members are kinesthetic and visual. They live through mobile technology. Put them in front of a desktop computer and they freeze. This generation has grown up *with* and *in* technology, which is as much a part of their lives as TV is to Generation X and radio is to Boomers. Gen Z is the true confluence of the three preceding generations: Gen Z grew up with a sense of group fear similar to Boomers; they will get the job done and work really hard like Generation X; and they live online like Millennials—yet they are the first generation to fear being alone and unconnected.

For interaction, they immerse themselves into a coded dimension. They will quickly adapt and use any technology that makes them part of a group (for example, FaceTime). Yet while they live online with each other, they still need the comfort of sitting together.

They need the physicality of being close to allay their fear of being alone. This group of young adults has never been alone because we trained them that way. If you can tell them how they will be rewarded and can prove you are worthy of their trust, they will put their heads down and get the job done. They trust freely, but with no conviction. They are cynical.

Gen Zers will change how the world works. They have never been without access to YouTube or Google. They think logically, are intelligent, and have no problem with difficult conversations—in their young lives, they have already had to have many about life, death, and money. This is the first generation to have gone to school in an environment where their very first lesson—called "lock-down"—was what to do if a bad person came into the school. This is the generation that hears daily about terrorists and sees their parents struggling to pay bills.

Listening Behavior Patterns: Text

Cues: Gen Zer's use memes, emojis, and "instastories."

Patterns: Tyler, like most of his generation, demonstrates a pattern of incredible intelligence but abbreviated communication. Gen Z has the shortest attention span of any of the generations. A smartphone was often their first form of entertainment. As their interactive generational anchoring benchmark suggests, they look for pictures, videos, and funny memes when "listening" on digital.

Listening Cues: Visual and Kinesthetic

This generation is the first generation to use a phone not just as a telephone but as a multipurpose communication device. As the first interactive generation, Gen Z is also the first generation to listen both visually and kinesthetically.

Email and Social Media Patterns: Memes

You will rarely receive an email from this generational cohort. Instead, you are more likely to receive a meme or text. This is the first generation since the advent of email to not use it as a primary source of communication. They prefer to group message or group text. They live by Facebook groups or Google Classroom to learn. Professors have had to send guidelines to these students on how to email them questions. When onboarding Gen Zers, companies find themselves having to explain what voicemail and email are and relay protocols for meeting conduct. This generation, even in grade school, has primarily communicated via text and Instagram, messages defined as short and to the point. Trying to get anyone in this cohort to pick up the phone is like pulling teeth. They would rather spend hours texting than talking—it's habit and it's easier.

Your emails to Gen Zers like Tyler should be short and structured. For example:

> **Salutation:** Not necessary.
>
> **Subject line:** "Tyler, can you help do . . ."
>
> **Body text:** Provide requirements, due dates, responsibilities, and clear direction. Include a link to a calendar invite.
>
> **Sign-off:** Not necessary, but you can always write, "Thanks, M" (your initial).

If your work culture is more formal, give them a template of how you email. For example, say, "We prefer formality, and here is how we do it." Encourage them with a calendar reminder to frequently check their emails. (They often forget about email as it is not their primary source of communication.)

How a Gen Zer Listens: Extreme Teaming

As part of the share-default group, this generation, like Millennials, thinks and shares constantly—it is in their nature. Because of their smartphones, they are the first generation to be in contact with people 24-7, and this is shaping how they process information and relationships. They have seen their parents work 24-7, and they see no problem with working outside the office. But they want to be connected with everyone and see how everyone else is working. They take what is now known as teaming to the next level. **Teaming** is a new term that denotes coming together as a team to achieve a goal. It never occurs to them that they should just email one person. They often send messages to a group. They grew up using technology like Google Classroom and are the first generation to think online education is the norm.

They are fully transparent, often sharing cell phone plans with their parents, who occasionally hear and see who they FaceTime with. However, after having grown up in the world of Wikileaks, Gen Zers realize the value of gaming and manipulating technology. This generation has changed everything with their ability to marshal Internet forces and intimidate their enemies. They are survivors who work hard, understand the relationship between work and money, and get stuff done when motivated by the process of work, not time.

Words and Phrases to Ensure You Are Heard

- Words that work best include "feel," "goals," "have a plan," and "love."

- Phrases to use to engage Gen Zers include "What do you believe?" and "Is this right or wrong?"

Digital Listening Stressors

- To improve your clarity, avoid stressors including "the Internet is down." This generation has never ever been without social media—they need their tribe to survive.

HOW CAN I DETERMINE MY TEAM'S PRIMARY LISTENING CUES?

Now that you understand how each generation communicates most effectively, it's important to understand how to operate when dealing with a multigenerational team. The best way to communicate is to address the largest generational cohort you have on the team and then manage up or down. Look for listening cues from your team to digitally mirror them.

I'll get to a fun test to try with your team, but before you get started, let's learn more about the visual auditory kinesthetic (VAK) system. VAK was first introduced by three professors in California in the 1960s who had a theory that children and adults have anchoring moments that are significant for absorbing and retaining information. The results of their research showed that different generations had different preferences when it came to communicating different messages. Today, VAK helps people identify their digital listening personalities or their primary and secondary preferences for communication.

The boxed item contains a quiz you can take with your team to discover their, and your, communication preferences. You can also take it first to determine your own digital mirroring preferences.

For this exercise, circle your answer as quickly as possible:

1. When seeking travel directions, I . . .

    A. use an app on my phone.

    B. ask someone for directions.

    C. follow my nose or maybe use a compass.

2. I tend to say . . .

    A. "I *see* what you mean."

    B. "I *hear* what you are saying."

    C. "I know how you *feel*."

3. To teach someone something, I . . .

    A. write instructions.

    B. explain verbally.

    C. demonstrate and let them have a try.

4. I tend to say . . .

    A. "*Watch* how I do it."

    B. "*Listen* to me explain this."

    C. "You try it yourself."

5. When choosing a new car I . . .

    A. read the reviews.

    B. discuss it with friends.

    C. test drive what I want.

6. I tend to say . . .

    A. "*Show* me."

     B. "*Tell* me."

     C. "Let me *try*."

7. I remember things best by . . .

     A. writing notes.

     B. saying words aloud or repeating them in my mind.

     C. doing and practicing the activity or imagining it being done.

To get your score, add up the number of letter responses:

    A: _____

    B: _____

    C: _____

Then look at the answer key here to determine your communication preferences:

    Mostly A = visual

    Mostly B = auditory

    Mostly C = kinesthetic

Your results are a snapshot of your current communication habits. This VAK test identifies what patterns your brain looks for, and connects with, most in order to reveal your primary and secondary preferences for communication.

Similarly, by being aware of your own communication preferences, you'll begin to notice patterns in coworkers' emails, presentations, texts, and even PowerPoints. These patterns are clues as to how your coworkers prefer to communicate. Consider the benefits for a new team member to take the VAK test and find out how their communication patterns should be adapted to the team's preferences. They could make, or break, a person's success.

IDENTIFY WHO IS ON YOUR TEAM

Throughout this chapter I have delivered a few different techniques to help you determine the makeup of your team, including:

- The VAK test to find out how you and others listen.

- Training your brain in listening preferences (use Table 1.2 to decode a message and respond accordingly).

- Looking for VAK patterns that help you identify a person's personality and generation and decide which tools to use.

But what I have found with my experience teaching is that often adult learners want a quick table that they can refer to (for example, in a photo or a printout they can put on their desk). Table 1.2 explains VAK, listening preferences, and patterns to help you quickly and easily determine the makeup of your team or any team you are working with.

TABLE 1.2: **Categorization and Digital Listening Patterns to Help You Reduce Assumptions**

Categorization	Ben the Boomer (Born 1945–1960)	Adam the Gen Xer (Born 1960–1980)	Trish the Millennial (Born 1980–2000)	Tyler the Gen Zer (Born 2000–2020)
GAB: Digital Listening	Formality (task default)	Get it done (task default)	Adapt or adopt (share default)	Interactive (share default)
Digital Listening Behavior Patterns	Well written	Goal based	Sticky notes	Text
Listening Cues	Auditory	Visual	Kinesthetic	Visual & kinesthetic
Email and Social Media Patterns	Letter	To-do list	SMS	Memes
How They Listen Best	Spitballing	Whiteboards	Teaming	Extreme teaming
Words and Phrases to Engage	"Tell me," "what I heard," "what you said"	"See," "snapshot," "perspective"	"Socialize," "you know," "pull some strings"	"Feel," "look," "like," "share," "see," "goals," "a plan"
Phrases That Inspire Engagement	"What is your opinion based on your experience?"	"Please help me picture this to make sure I have a better understanding."	"What do you think? How can we adapt or improve this?"	"What do you believe?"
Digital Listening Stressors	Not discussing	"No, you won't"	"You can't"	No Internet

In addition, use Table 1.3 to craft perfect emails according to who you are communicating with:

TABLE 1.3: **How to Write Emails to Reduce Digital Static**

Part of Email	Boomers (Born 1945–1960)	Gen Xers (Born 1960–1980)	Millennials (Born 1980–2000)	Gen Zers (Born 2000–2020)
Introduction	"Dear [first name],"	First name	"Hey [first name],"	No salutation
Subject Line	Detailed	Short, concise overview	Action required	Text
Content	Well-written, in paragraph format. Indicate action required. Due date for completion. Attach docs.	Overview in bullet-point format. Indicate action required. Due date for completion. Attach docs.	Indicate action required with due date for completion. Overview with links to support docs.	Share Google docs. Provide due date in a calendar.

The patterns introduced in this chapter will help eliminate the voices in your head, but how do you begin fostering stronger relationships through your digital conversation? By building digital trust, being like Google, and copying Chester Barnard, as you'll learn in the next chapter.

CHAPTER TWO

STEP 2:
ELIMINATE DIGITAL DISTRUST

DIGITAL DISTRUST AND WHY IT HAPPENS

How much do you trust in your ability to do your work? Would you give a 100 percent guarantee to your team and your customers that you would be at your *very best* every day, no matter what? Business management theory, and simple common sense, would say that as hard as people try to be at their best, being at their very best all the time isn't possible. No one would have the gall to make such a guarantee.

But one company did, and it caught the attention of Christopher Hart, who wrote about it in *Harvard Business Review* in 1988. In the article, he describes the huge success "Bugs" Burger Bug Killers (BBBK)—a Miami-based pest-extermination company now owned by S. C. Johnson & Son—had with a service guarantee. BBBK promised hotels that it would eliminate all their pests, and they didn't have to pay for the service until they were sure the pests were gone. Then BBBK went further: if hotel guests found a pest after BBBK performed its services, the company would write the guests a letter taking full responsibility and pay for their dinners and their rooms or a future stay. BBBK then went even one step further. If one of the company's hotel clients was closed down due to pests after its services, BBBK would pay *all* fines and give the client $5,000. Because of this service guarantee, BBBK—which is still in business today, 32 years after the article was written—charges the highest fees in its business for its services, has a huge share of the market, and has made a substantial profit.

The author of the article states BBBK's "service quality is so outstanding that the company rarely needs to make good on its guarantee. In 1986 it paid out only $120,000 on sales of $33 million—just enough to prove that its promises aren't empty ones."[1] The owner and founder of BBBK, Mr. Burger (his son now owns the business), built trust not only with his customers but with his employees and within his community. Mr. Burger invested his profits back into his team based on their tenure, and he did outstanding volunteer work in his community. He built trust capital and in doing so enabled his business, employees, and community to flourish. Trust capital is like savings in a bank: it builds up over time, and if you make a mistake, you have a higher chance of being forgiven.

Trust is a profitable endeavor, but the challenge today is building trust with digital. Digital communication and media are to trust what oil is to water—digital communication sinks trust, just as oil sinks water. Trust is believing in the reliability of the information provided. According to a global study conducted by Ernst & Young in 2018, "less than half of global professionals trust their employer, boss or team/colleagues,"[2] and without trust, we cannot be engaged or productive. The cure to this problem is to build trust though clear messaging that aligns with how each generation trusts digitally, because when you build trust, you increase performance.

In my first business, one of my partners was an honorably discharged Navy SEAL. His mantra was "high-quality performance results in high profit." He would drill into my head that trusted communication is the foundation for teams, businesses, and innovation. He explained that when he was in action with his SEAL team, he had to trust in orders; trust that every member of the team was going to do what they were ordered to do; and trust that each team member had each other's back. He explained that during missions, he often couldn't see where he was going or what was coming, but he could hear his team members giving him directions through his headphones. He had to trust the words he was hearing to get the job done. He also had to trust that his people would do the right thing if the wrong thing happened.

Both the SEALs and BBBK understand that trust is the key to great performance, and the experts agree. According to the article "The Connection between Employee Trust and Financial Performance," Stephen M. R. Covey and Douglas R. Conant believe that trust is paramount to good business. They explain that there is a very strong connection between trust and financial performance. Your ability to build trust has a profound effect on business results because trust affects two measurable outcomes: speed and cost. When trust goes down (in a relationship, on a team, in an organization, or with a partner or customer), speed goes down and cost goes up.[3]

We know that teams fail if the team members don't trust each other, so the big question is, how do you build that trust? If we go back in time, we will see that we have faced this issue of trust and technology before. Let's explore that history and meet Chester Barnard.

TRUST AND PRODUCTIVITY

Chester Barnard understood that trust increased productivity both internally and externally. He was president of Bell Telephone in the 1930s, and he realized that his people were focusing too much on the task of making sales and not enough on helping customers trust the new technology the company was selling. At that time, Barnard and his team were selling a new technology called the telephone, but people were afraid it would be a time-waster in the workplace. People have always hated change, and executives would come up with excuses not to buy the telephone.

After graduating from Harvard, Barnard got a job as a statistical clerk at the American Telephone and Telegraph Company, now AT&T, in Boston, and he stayed there for most of his career. Eventually, he became the president of the New Jersey Bell Telephone Company, part of AT&T. As president, his first priority was to get his employees to trust him and his new model of management, called the acceptance theory of authority. Barnard and other researchers—including Elton Mayo, Douglas McGregor, Edward Deming, and eventually the great management guru Peter Drucker—believed the exact opposite of what previous executives and academics believed about management theory. These acceptance theorists, including Barnard, believed it was important for employees to trust leadership. Previous management styles didn't consider employee trust—employees were paid to work, not to trust.

Barnard believed that employees considered the validity of a leader's orders and then decided consciously whether to accept them or not. A directive was accepted by the employees if they understood it, were able to follow it, and believed it related to their goals and their understanding of the organization's goals. In management theory, this time is considered the beginning of the human transitional era of management. Workers became valuable assets rather than a drag on profit and loss statements. Leaders of this era believed in what Kurt Lewin found in his research in 1939: behavior is a function of people and the environment.[4] Trust in messaging is key to a productive culture. To develop trust with a still shell-shocked generation of workers, sell phones, and create success for his clients and his company, Barnard created the first "cool" workplace.

Barnard let his employees operate in a mode that helped them be productive *and* creative. He built trust through clear communication that demonstrated he didn't just talk the talk but also walked the walk. For example, in 1933, at the height of the Great Depression, Barnard announced a no-layoff policy—a major achievement even within the Bell System—choosing to reduce employees' working hours instead.[5]

People tested him. They rode unicycles down the office corridors—yet his messaging never varied. He encouraged them to be themselves. His memos didn't talk about him; they talked about the people who worked for him and the changes they could manifest. Eventually, he talked about how to build the same sense of trust with clients. All of this was unheard of in the 1930s. His was a Google workplace before Google. He reduced people's lack of trust by shifting his communication to meet their needs. He didn't say, "I will fire you if you don't meet my goals." When business was bad, he didn't threaten people, and he didn't take away all of their jobs' perks. When he had to take away some perks, he explained why. He was transparent and clear.

Chester Barnard believed you can only lead when people can understand what you say, follow it, and believe it will help them *and* the organization. That's a really, really important point because it has become the definition of digital trust. People can only communicate clearly and accurately through digital technology when they have the ability to understand the message you are sending them, no matter the technical medium. They must then believe that if they act upon your messaging, or respond to you, what they do, or will be doing, will help them get their job, project, or goals accomplished, which will in turn help the team or organization.

Rarely does leadership's digital communication meet these criteria. Leaders often assume people know what is in it for themselves and the organization. Yet quite the contrary is true. As research from the UK's Crowe Associates Ltd.,[6] *Harvard Business Review*,[7] and many other sources proves, people do not trust leaders. If you do not convey a message in a way your people can understand it and then follow through on it to achieve *their* goals, they will not trust either you or your message. Barnard realized that to get his people to sell, innovate, and manage clients, they could not be afraid of losing their jobs or their perceived power. He also realized different team members needed different cues to align with a leader. So in our multigenerational workplace, what are the cues for trust? Let's find out.

TRUST CUES FOR THE DIGITAL WORKPLACE

To be like Barnard and build digital trust among your teams, you must send clear messages and be known as someone who is trustworthy. The key is to know how a team member will trust your message. You must know how to send them information in a format that helps them problem solve or get a job done. Here is an example from my friend, client, and mentor Samy.

Samy is an experienced and talented leader with a diverse generational sales team. During one of their last quarters for the year, he encouraged his folks to "make goal." He knew in his gut that something else was missing in his approach, but he didn't know what. I suggested my training could help his team identify how both they and their clients trust others. Understanding how to build trust would increase the call-to-close rate. Although this was an unusual time for training, Samy gave the program a shot.

The results? Not only did Samy's team meet their sales targets, they exceeded them. Team performance was enhanced by understanding how to build digital trust with their clients. When my team and I asked his team what made the difference between the sales they had just completed and other assignments, they told us, "We felt we had 10 percent more time, and we were really able to spend that on our clients' problems rather than engage in the back and forth of email or phone tag."

What Samy did was utilize my *Success Together* course to give his team the tools to build trust. Within the course I teach people how to use the **triangle of digital trust**, illustrated in Figure 2.1:

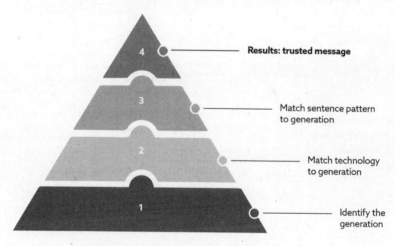

FIGURE 2.1: The Triangle of Digital Trust

HOW TO UTILIZE THE TRIANGLE OF DIGITAL TRUST

To build digital trust in your messaging, you can use the triangle of digital trust. To use this system, start by classifying the generations you are dealing with. Then determine how they use technology and their default technology, such as Google Docs, Slack, or email. Once you have determined this information, you can determine the correct sentence pattern or structure to employ (the email templates in Chapter 1 can help you create your message). And as a result of each step, as the top of the triangle of digital trust shows, you will be able to categorize and recognize the technology and pattern to clarify your message and build trust.

By fine-tuning your use of technology, you will reduce the barrier of misunderstanding that leads to mistrust. Figure 2.2 shows the generational anchoring benchmarks and patterns that will help you do exactly that.

Technology Anchors	Boomers Born 1945–1960	Gen Xers Born 1960–1980	Millennials Born 1980–2000	Gen Zers Born 2000–2020
Born into Technology	Radio	TV	Computer	Share and savvy
Adaptive Technology	TV	Computer	Share	Lock and share
Technology: Self	Forced to learn for work	Used in isolation to share with others	Group socialization	Group knowledge

Cues and Prompts

Technology and Learning	Calculators and typewriters	Computers	Group work (Facebook groups)	Group work with shared documents
Technology and Team	Worked in isolation, supported team	Worked on personal computers for team	Teamwork with technology	Team is technology
Technology and Disruptors	Loss of dialogue	Loss of human association	No sharing	Not linked
How to Engage	Call them, talk to them, leave a voicemail	Get them together as a group; allow them to brainstorm and report	Develop them with learning; let them "like," be liked, and learn	Provide opportunities to share and learn

FIGURE 2.2: Generational Anchoring Benchmarks: Trust

GENERATIONAL ANCHORING BENCHMARKS: TRUST

The generational anchoring benchmarks around trust and technology are derived from common generational experiences and patterns in school and early in one's career. Trust anchors help people frame problems, solutions, and encounters they experience using technology. These anchors are like spellcheck for problem solving: they help you clarify for your audience what's in it for them, the organization, and you. This enables you to build digital trust.

Digital Trust Anchors for Ben and Other Boomers

Ben, our Boomer, had an exceptional introduction to the workforce. When he entered his first job, companies were expanding, the economy was ticking along, and you could get a job (potentially for life) when you graduated from high school. Boomers worked in the era before shareholder value became a quarterly obsession. They learned from leaders and were allowed to make mistakes on the job.

As we learned in the previous chapter, Boomers grew up in an auditory era. Television was in its infancy, and people listened to the radio; they therefore appreciate "language" and value face-to-face communication. They are engaged by, and trust in, a leader who follows protocol yet takes the time to meet the team. Gaining a Boomer's trust takes time. It is a give-and-take activity driven by the sound of productivity. As children, Boomers had to converse. Their parents expected them to talk while at the dinner table. Consequently, they became great conversationalists, and they develop relationships through talking. When they were teenagers, the telephone was the technology they used to share news.

This generation was led by a strict paramilitary code. Schools had truant officers, offices had clock-in machines, and great ethical leaders were celebrated. This code was grounded in the belief that the leader leads and the followers do what the leader demands. But before you can convince Boomers to follow you, you first have to gain their trust.

One of the most interesting points found in the data from my research is how much Boomers are prepared to trust a leader. Boomers reported not only trusting their leaders but learning from them. Boomers expect to receive a direct command from a leader. They enjoy hearing or writing about how this command is going to help them build or better the organization.

My uncle Jim, whom I mentioned in the previous chapter, is a Boomer who has always appreciated and respected leadership. When he had team meetings, he was very comfortable sitting at the head of the table, and as the leader, he led the conversation and listened intently when his team spoke. He didn't take notes, but even days later, he could repeat the conversation and was able to distill the issues at hand into a few clear and concise paragraphs. He was an auditory learner. His use of technology reflects this, as does Ben's and that of almost every Boomer I met during my research.

My research found that, today, Boomers love the cell phone for its convenience and prefer to use it to talk rather than text. To build trust with Ben and the Boomers in your workplace, you must understand the best ways to specifically and continuously build trust, which include the following.

Digital Trust Triggers for Boomers

- **Personal alignment:** When you message Boomers, be respectful. They appreciate the chain of command. Boomers experience leadership as a monarchy. To engage a Boomer, align your message with the mission of the organization. If a timely response isn't given, call them and encourage a discussion.

- **Rewards:** Having put in the hard work, Boomers want to secure their legacy. They are prepared and, in most cases, have dedicated their lives to their work. But they also expect their reward to be a pension and the ability to care for themselves long after leaving the workplace, which is exactly what they were promised when they began working.

- **Team alignment and company mission:** Boomers are often prepared to make great sacrifices for company's mission.

Messaging Tips to Build Trust with Boomers

- Boomers appreciate dialogue when it comes to leadership, and lack of trust occurs when dialogue is lost. Don't be afraid to Skype or FaceTime with this group. Although they enjoy a phone call, they have adapted to the technology that enables them to see others on a call. This is a witty group; they enjoy a good debate. If you are not connecting with the Boomers on your team, meet with them or call them. Talk to them.

- Do not be afraid of messing up and looking bad with this generation. Boomers learned from trying and failing.

- Boomers frame the context of a problem based on the company's culture and mission.

- Boomers are results oriented and motivated by security.

Digital Trust Anchors for Adam and Other Gen Xers

When Adam entered the workforce, the world was changing. Star CEOs, junk bonds, the Enron scandal, and the growing opulence of the CEO parachute were all the rage. Gen X experienced leadership that had directly departed from the management theory of Chester Barnard and Peter Drucker to a more laissez-faire, or anything goes, management model, one that believed the essence of leadership was "it all depends." In this model, the situation was balanced with the relationship. A leader's style would determine the extent to which this balance was achieved; leaders therefore became the focus, and employees became numbers on a P&L statement that shareholders reviewed. People I interviewed called this the end of the "gold watch era" of work. Employers didn't care about you or what you had done—they cared about shareholders and shareholder value because that was what their salaries were based on, versus developing culture or employees.

Governments and organizations everywhere were dealing with deficits. Growing up and living through recessions shaped Gen X's trust triggers. They went through many: the recession of 1973–1975; the 1980s, which had more bankruptcies than any previous decade and experienced a continual rise in interest rates; the dot-com bust of 1995–2001; and the great recession of 2007–2008. For this generation, money became the key to trust.

Gen Xers were taught that they had to *lean in* (before the phrase was a thing) to leaders, but a funny thing happened while they were *leaning in* in their youth—they were thrown under the bus. They believe that whoever is in control has all of the responsibility. And all of these trust triggers have been reinforced by their visual entertainment, including movies (such as Oliver Stone's *Wall Street*, mentioned in the Introduction), the news (which included the first all-news TV station, CNN), and the rise of Martha Stewart and the picture-perfect life.

They are the most money-focused of all generations, because as they were coming of age, the idea of lifetime pensions or healthcare was dying. You had to manage your 401k and make career decisions that benefited you. This drove Gen X to be very independent. Gen Xers are the command-and-control team members of your group. Gen Xers process learning from leaders through command-and-control systems. They take the command from their leaders, put their heads down, and take control of the project or mission.

When Gen Xers interact with a leader, they read, listen, and respond with an ear for self- and team-preservation. They operate by asking questions internally, such as "What is the vision?" "How is this going to help me?" and "What do I have to do to achieve the results you (my manager) need, which will enable me to get my reward?"

Today, Gen Xers work for leaders, but they do not trust them, as our data on Gen Xers demonstrate. Leadership development was placed second after shareholder returns, so Gen Xers were either held back or given positions of responsibility without the right tools or the right compensation. What made matters worse, when Gen X was coming of age in the workplace, the idea of the CEO golden parachute was developed, which meant that no matter how poorly CEOs managed a company, they could walk away (or be told to walk away) with rich rewards from a failing company.

To develop trust with Gen Xers, give them the ability to run their own show and report back to you but don't micromanage them or use threats against them. Although Gen Xers have a right to be cynical and unhappy, many really enjoy working hard and being responsible—it is in their DNA.

Digital Trust Triggers for Gen Xers

- **Personal alignment:** As in their university days, when you need to build trust with Gen Xers, get them together and allow them to brainstorm. If a group setting is not possible, use email and include social proof of the messaging in the form of a PowerPoint. If you need to increase motivation for a Gen X team, do not pull punches. This is the command-and-control generation; if you message that they have the power to get a project done, they will take the reins and just do it.

- **Rewards:** Meeting or exceeding KPIs means getting a reward. In the case of Gen X, that means money. In our data, my team and I found that most Gen Xers began to disengage from their leaders when a change in reward was made. For example, take two sales teams: one team hits its target and expects to be bonused as promised, and the other team does not hit its target. The VP of sales decides no one receives a bonus. Good salespeople begin to leave the company.

- **Team alignment and company mission:** Gen Xers align with the organization's vision. They prefer to picture the good of the organization and the possibilities of their teams.

Messaging Tips to Build Trust with Gen Xers

Adam and his fellow Gen Xer friends were the last generation to really enjoy college. As shown in the previous chapter, unlike Millennials and Gen Zers, Gen Xers didn't have to focus on grades with the same fixation that students do now and in the two generations prior. This generation had fun being together and learning.

- When you need this group to learn and trust each other, get them together in person, have food, and give them a whiteboard and notebook, or better yet, provide technology that combines both.

- As a leader, you will have a tough time engaging this generation. Gen Xers are naturally suspicious. Use visual check-ins with this group. In a meeting with Gen Xers, use a chart and say something along the lines of "I said I would do this; this is what I have done; and this is how it will affect you."

- If there is bad news, tell them right away and tell them whether or not you have a plan. Gen Xers are familiar with difficult circumstances. They can handle bad news, but they disengage when they are kept in the dark.

- They are task managers. Technology is for work, not for play. Tell them where you are in a project or a decision or they will automatically mistrust you. They want to know if you have accomplished what you said you would do, and if not, they will ask, "Why not?" This group is more Jack Welch than Chester Barnard. Welch is known for saying "it isn't about you . . ." Chester is famous for saying "it's all about you . . ." At work, Gen Xers worry more about the bottom line than technology. Once the strategy has been created, they will keep the team on task. Often, Gen Xers are so focused on getting the job done, they will force the "What have you done for us lately?" conversation.

- They expect benchmarks, and they work to plan. Always being "first hired and first fired," they know that if they get the job done, they get paid. If they don't get the job done, they are fired.

Digital Trust Anchors for Trish and Other Millennials

Trish and her fellow Millennials process trust in leaders and corporations through the eyes of their peers, social media, and according to how the leaders live the "ethics of the brand."

There are three misconceptions I often hear about Millennials: one, they are lazy; two, they spend all their time on their phones; and three, all they do is question directions when they should just do what they are told. Let me respond to these by first saying that a lack of trust in the "traditional way" of doing things underscores Millennials' actions.

First, Millennials aren't lazy; they have been brought up to be self-confident and self-aware. When they don't see the value of accomplishing a task, they look to figure out how they can change it. They have cocareers with their parents, who help them with everything from negotiating contracts to deciding when to step away from work. They saw their parents work themselves to the bone only to lose in the 2007–2008 great recession, and they saw firsthand how trust was broken. They continue to see it today, so they are cautious in who they "kill" themselves for at work.

Second, Millennials live on their phones because they have learned to trust their peer groups and they share everything with their friends. No matter what you, as a leader, tell them, they will go online to verify the information and then use a social network to double-check that those facts are true. This is very frustrating for some leaders, as they have never had employees who do this and who cannot accept things at face value. Facebook, LinkedIn, Twitter, Instagram—all those wonderful things—are very much like the telephone was to Chester Barnard's workers—they are how Millennials communicate.

Finally, Millennials question directions because, as a group, that is what they were taught to do: question, challenge, be curious. This was the main parenting strategy in the '80s, and this generation was given choices. "What do you want to wear?" "What do you want for lunch?" "How about this or that?" Boomers' and Gen Xers' parents, on the other hand, ordered their children what to wear, and they decided what their children would eat for lunch.

Digital Trust Triggers for Millennials

- **Personal alignment:** Millennials experience leaders as an exercise in trust. They are not as naturally cynical as the generation before them or the one now coming after them. If you can earn their trust, they will fully engage, and that engagement will build a solid, profitable business.

- **Rewards:** This generation enjoys work and its benefits, but they love experiencing life. Change your method of reward assessment from "task" to "time." If you work in a unionized environment, it is important to recognize this changing trend and ask Millennials how to make it work as part of the collective bargaining process. They will surprise you. Work-life balance, not money, is the reward for learning. They have adapted to the new realities of the digital workplace. They know they can work at any time, from anywhere, which means they are organized and their calendar is their life. They value *time for living* and build it into their daily routine.

- **Team alignment and company mission:** Vision and mission are old-fashioned. Millennials respect organizations that live the brand's ethos, morals, and ethics.

Messaging Tips to Build Trust with Millennials

- "TL;DR" stands for "too long; didn't read." Millennials are so busy and, as a result, may ignore a long email. But a quick, clear calendar invite that includes resources will help them plot out how to get the job done. Today, your environment sends the message of how you respect and trust your team. Have Millennials work in groups, not in cubicles. They need to share how they have processed information, and they will share their sources. Millennials have the ability to adapt to almost any team. They love to share and discuss ideas online. They compare and contrast answers using multiple online sources. Put this talent to use to help you innovate new products.

- When trying to motivate and direct members of this generation, you will have a tough time if you just give them orders, especially without putting those orders into context. Instead, align what needs to get done with the ethos of your organization. Create a moral or ethical team code and then follow it. But be warned—if you break it, they will leave.

- When creating a team, give members the opportunity to determine their *code of behavior*. What are the rules of the team? How does the team operate? And what happens if you do not follow the rules?

- If there is bad news, they will find it, so it is best to be up front if something bad is going to happen or has happened. Tell them how it affects the team and the brand. Trying to hide information from them is fruitless.

- Allow them time to test but continually remind them of deadlines. This is best done through calendar reminders.

Digital Trust Anchors for Tyler and Other Gen Zers

Tyler and his Gen Z cohort are capable of building trust like no other generation. They will trust leaders based on their digital history. Gen Zers are visual and kinesthetic learners, but they trust digitally.

Gen Zers will read your history. They will know your faults and missteps because they will find them. Instagram, Snapchat, and Tik-Tok all feed their need to connect while also building a foothold for trust digitally and globally. Because of social media, Gen Zers have friends from all over the world who help them and chat with them.

As can be seen in the aftermath of numerous school shootings, 13- and 14-year-old children sadly, but strongly, know that the pen is mightier than the sword. Their weapon of rebellion isn't a gun; it's destroying others through digital means. They will use social media to expose the truth. One example, shared throughout the news after a school shooting, is when a group of Gen Zers shared information online about people who were trying to thwart their demands to get guns off the streets. They "dug" into people's social media profiles and shared information about these people that the pro-gun lobby didn't like.

Like Millennials, they don't accept people at face value. They will check you out, and then if you are consistent in your platform, they will begin to trust you.

Unlike other generations, they multitask naturally, but this affects their learning because they have shorter attention spans. They consume information in short bursts. Think about a half-hour TV sitcom, which usually consists of about 22 minutes of content. Gen Zers get bored in less than 22 minutes' time because they are used to YouTube. According to research by the University of Ottawa, "For them, the internet is not technology: it's a normal part of life. XML replaces HTML: merely viewing the web becomes changing it."[8]

My data on Gen Zers and their relationship to leaders is thin, as they are still on the cusp of entering the workforce, but early indications are that Gen Zers will be the Sherlock Holmes of the work world. Like the famous detective, Gen Zers naturally look for clues of alignment with their leaders, including their professors. They look for online patterns in leaders and in an organization's brand that will feed their need to accomplish something with purpose. Early research suggests this generation will be hardworking and value money, much like their Depression-era great-great-grandparents. However, unlike their great-great-grandparents, they will be transparent about money. Gen Zers grew up in a recession and with WikiLeaks, so they want leadership that will be fully transparent about their work and the work of others.

Gen Zers are reflective. They quietly consult their phones for information and then react. They work alone but interact with groups through their smartphones. They need the physical contact and stimulation from others. They want to know that a workspace and a leader are safe. Like the generation before them, they look for a digital trail that offers clues to the organization's moral and ethical code.

Like their great-grandparents, this generation has had more bad news in their short lives than any other before them. It is hard to find a Gen Zer who has not been personally affected by a random shooter (either at school or elsewhere), suicide, or cyberbullying. As a result, they are very resilient. This generation deals with bad news quickly and well. They create action plans with their friends online to protect themselves. This generation, along with Millennials, will usher in a return to Chester Barnard's style of leadership focused on relationships. They believe in the power of clear, succinct messaging and management that builds trust in their teams. They will flock to innovative new companies that have embraced this type of management and leadership.

Digital Trust Triggers for Gen Zers

- **Personal alignment:** Gen Zers experience leaders online. They expect daily updates about the company through social media. This generation has never had to wait for information before, so they don't expect to wait for information from a leader now. Give them daily feedback *and* the opportunity to give daily feedback in return, as the company Glint.com offers.

- **Rewards:** Money, then time. They also manage money through time: "If I do this, how long will it take until I get that?" Using their smartphones, they work 24-7, resting when they feel they deserve it. Many of them learned this from their Gen X parents who were always on their phones, demonstrating to their children that work is the most important aspect of life at home. And this generation can manage themselves well.

- **Team alignment and company mission:** Information and ethics are their priorities. Ensure Gen Zers are never in the dark. Like Sherlock Holmes, they will find the light and flee. They check online to see how others have dealt with a problem they need to solve or attained a goal they would like to achieve. YouTube is the top search engine for this group.

Messaging Tips to Build Trust with Gen Zers

- Prove you're not a liar. Gen Z is the first generation to experience life online. They hunt and apply for jobs or university courses using tools such as Glassdoor.com and Ratemyprofessor.com, which were developed by Millennials. They are driven by algorithms. Gen Z manipulates these algorithms by writing the words in their résumés that the job application asks for. That's how they get to the next stage. When they finally get offered the interview, before they go, they research the company through social media, but not the trending media like Instagram—they use the tried-and-true LinkedIn.

- All things old are new again. This generation is fascinated with old-fashioned daily timers, and they like the tactile quality of writing with pens and pencils and creating a calendar they can hold in their hands. Of course, they do take pictures of their calendar to share on social media and still keep an "old-fashioned" online calendar.

- Tell them when something needs to be done and what the rules are, then leave them alone to get it done.

BREAKING THROUGH THE BARRIER
OF DIGITAL TRUST

With all of this knowledge, you can build trust through your digital communication. Once you break through this barrier, you will be able to motivate your team to accomplish tasks more quickly. Now that you are busting through the barrier of mistrust, let's explore how you can customize and continue to build trust. Then let's see how, like BBBK, you can use this knowledge to grow your business and create a culture that enables everyone in your culture, and your client community, to thrive and make money.

CHAPTER THREE

STEP 3: UNDERSTAND MISUNDERSTANDINGS

THE PROBLEM WITH DIGITAL FEEDBACK

Whether we are giving feedback or receiving feedback, it is hard. You personally know this, but my research backs it up. We will discuss why it is difficult to give and receive feedback, but interestingly enough, it is harder to do through email than it is in person—10 times harder to be exact. We perceive feedback as 90 percent negative when it comes to us digitally. This perception causes anxiety, and it is difficult to act on.

Dr. Clifford Nass, author of *The Man Who Lied to His Laptop*, has found that negative feedback consumes more of our intellectual energy than positive feedback. Our brains think about negative feedback more than they do about positive feedback. It's logical to then conclude digital feedback can take people off task. When we receive a text, an email, or a direct message (DM) about something positive regarding our work, we smile and move on. But when we receive an email or text that we don't understand, we perceive it as negative. We think about it, we think about it more, we dwell on it, and then we react negatively, completely forgetting the positive messages that we have received.

Without feedback, we aren't the best we can be. To see feedback for what it is—*a tool to help us get better*—it's important to be aware of the fact that our brains have been conditioned to see digital feedback as negative, and we must actively work to recondition our brains to recognize patterns in digital feedback.

But why do we see digital feedback as negative feedback? The answer has to do with the different hemispheres of our brains. Negative information generally involves additional thinking, and according to Dr. Nass, it is often processed much more thoroughly than positive thoughts.[1] When we see, read, or experience negative feedback, we tend to think more about that feedback than any positive feedback. Mr. Ríos, the CEO of Happyforce, a software communications company, brought this into focus on his blog. He wrote that when using his software, one of his clients only saw the small percentage of positive feedback on leadership because her brain was trying to process the negative feedback. We all do this. As Mr. Ríos explains, "Our brains respond to negative digital feedback like it's a death threat."[2]

It isn't public speaking or even death we fear most—it is getting feedback, especially when received digitally. We naturally want to protect ourselves from negativity. We want to see the feedback on our projects and the emails that come our way as positive, but instead we see only the small percentage of negative feedback—and we obsess over it. One Millennial in our research shared how she obsessed over negative feedback so much that she almost lost her new job.

After a rather rocky start with her boss, Jennifer felt that all communication with her boss was negative. She was consumed by what she perceived as negative feedback. She would constantly go back to her phone and reread not only the feedback but the entire conversation thread. She found herself reading into every word, and she even looked at the time the messages were sent and how long her boss took to respond to her.

As Dr. Nass found, we obsess over negative feedback. Digital just makes it easier to misunderstand or assume.

THE FEEDBACK WASTELAND

Employees crave feedback. But feedback and tools for providing feedback have become a garbage heap of trial and error. Employees want feedback but see the digital feedback they get from their managers as negative. This requires the manager to clarify things, which takes the manager off task and takes even more time. Then the employees get stressed and disengage.

I asked one of the members of our research group, Tony, if he had ever seen the downside of using digital communication as a feedback tool. "Oh yes," he said. He continued:

> If I could figure out how to actually go and see everyone I need to give feedback to in person, my productivity would be off the charts. Instead, no matter what I do to give constructive feedback digitally, it often goes offside, and I have to spend my time helping them understand what I meant.

And Tony's company requires him to give his team members feedback on their performance every quarter.

Performance management has shifted. In the past, corporations gave performance feedback once a year. Writing in *Harvard Business*

Review, Peter Cappelli and Anna Tavis explain that today, "employers are also finally acknowledging that both supervisors and subordinates despise the appraisal process."[3]

Compounding this problem is that less than 10 percent of corporations understand how to deal with the challenge that is digital performance management. According to a *Harvard Business Review* article by Christine Porath, high-performing teams share nearly six times more positive feedback than average teams. Meanwhile, low-performing teams share nearly twice as much negative feedback as average teams.[4]

Jose, a seasoned Gen X leader at a Fortune Top 10 company, knows these facts and is frustrated by the migration to digital feedback. When I called and asked him if his feedback process works digitally, he said, "It doesn't. Someone always misunderstands me, and then it just goes south. If you can give me a solution, I would appreciate it." I taught Jose a generational feedback loop to help him, and the results speak for themselves. Not only did Jose sharpen his own digital feedback skills, he used the generational feedback loop with his team.

The importance of feedback for a leader's development can never be underestimated, as the following quote from my research highlights:

> Feedback is a very important step for a leader to be able to improve and keep evolving. As a leader, getting negative feedback would allow you to think about the current situation and keep changing in the right way to be able to adapt to others and improve operations. Feedback should be able to come from either the team you lead or your managers. From what I have been able to see, if leaders fear negative feedback they will not be able to overcome the difficulties, and it will become a daily challenge. Getting

feedback allows you to keep a sane relationship with your peers and working out negative ones give you the opportunity to get better. Communication is the key, so leaders should always be able to give and receive feedback.

USE A DIGITAL FEEDBACK LOOP

A feedback loop is designed to change a behavior. It gives you information or data in real time (for example, about your performance or health). Once you get the data, you have the opportunity to improve your performance or behavior. Technology, offices, and software use a feedback loop, and you may even use one when you are running on a treadmill. On a treadmill, you can wear a heart monitor that indicates your heart rate, and the readout on the treadmill shows your speed. You use these feedback metrics to improve your performance, and that feedback changes your behavior.

When we give feedback in person, as in my Jose example, we choose where we are going to give the feedback and how we are going to give it, considering our tone of voice and our body language (for example, arms folded or arms on our desk). Then we wait to see how the person responds to this feedback. We take in their verbal and physical signals, and we either continue along or shift gears. But how do we do this digitally? We use technology for what it is—a mirror of our preferences. For example, Gen Zers like Snapchat because the messages sent disappear. Gen Xers like email because they can see a trail of productivity. Both are examples of digital body language.

DIGITAL BODY LANGUAGE

Your **digital body language** is probably something you don't think about often, if ever, yet it is the biggest trigger for digital feedback.

Part of your digital body language is the technology you choose to give digital feedback. It's not what you say but how you say it. It either engages people or enrages them, similar to how people react to body language in person.

When I was explaining the concept of digital body language in New York City, a brash and intelligent 20-something stood up and, as only a true New Yorker could, yelled out, "Great! Now, could you please teach my boss phone etiquette?" Somewhat surprised, given I was speaking to a group of professional service workers, I asked for more details. The young professional explained, "He doesn't know how to use a phone. He leaves me *voicemails*!" Gen Xers and Boomers (and I) burst out laughing, as did the 20-something, but the crux of the problem was real. This employee felt that his boss was nagging him and giving him negative feedback because his boss used voicemail when, in fact, his boss was on the road all the time and thought leaving a voicemail was a quicker and more efficient way of communicating.

Every day, we experience digital body language—yet we just don't know how to categorize it. So I'd like to do that now. Digital body language includes the technology you choose to deliver the message, the words you choose, the order of your words, the rhythm of your writing, and the pace. For example, when I give my daughter feedback on a paper she is writing for school, she uses primarily one-word texts to respond to me. When my editor gives me feedback, I tend to respond in an email with abbreviated sentences of up to 10 words. When my mom gives me feedback on my writing, she calls me. Then, after leaving a voicemail, she sends me an email that includes full sentences, never uses abbreviations, and is always grammatically correct, just as in her not-so-frequent texts. (She is a great editor, btw.) Like the women in my family, each of us has our own unique digital body language, and if we can understand this language better, we can begin to defeat the barrier of digital feedback.

Before we dive into the specifics of each generation, take a look at Figure 3.1 for a general overview of each generation's predisposition for digital body language, based on its anchoring benchmarks for feedback and productivity.

GENERATIONAL ANCHORING BENCHMARKS: DIGITAL BODY LANGUAGE

Triggers	Boomers Born 1945–1960	Gen Xers Born 1960–1980	Millennials Born 1980–2000	Gen Zers Born 2000–2020
Digital Body Language	Dignified	Strong	Appealing	Enchanting
Goal of Body Language	I want to influence others	I want to influence outcome	We want to work to influence the group—and the world	We want to influence change
Self View	Big thinker	Fix problems by deconstruction	Build through design (like Picasso)	Build through technology (like Steve Jobs)
Stress Indicator	Disruptors	Bottlenecks	The fidget	The fixated

Cues and Prompts

	Boomers	Gen Xers	Millennials	Gen Zers
To Reduce Negative Response Conditioning	Use formal language and face-to-face interactions	Use e-comms and straight talk; present facts	Use positive, motivational, fun-type e-comms (e.g., cell phones, email, IM, text)	Video and sharing
Phrases That Motivate	"We value you"; "You are needed by our leader"	"Please do it your way—throw away the rules"	"Your team will include other intelligent, creative folks"	"This will help you do X"; "It will help your teammates"
Their Value to the Team	Cultural capital	Intellectual capital	Communication capital	Technology capital

FIGURE 3.1: Generational Anchoring Benchmarks: Digital Body Language

Digital body language is the message you communicate digitally, but not through your words. Just as our physical body language is nonverbal, such as a head nod in agreement or an eye roll, digital body language is nonverbal, and it is based on each individual's personal interpretations and experiences.

Let's see how digital body language plays out across each generation so we can make sure the messages we send are the messages received.

Ben the Boomer

When Ben was in school, the technology he worked with was pen and paper, along with a typewriter and a calculator. His learning devices and environment were loud. He heard teachers give feedback and was in a classroom where discussion, debate, and questions and answers filled the air. It was the sound of productivity. As Ben got older, when he walked into the typing pool (a group of secretaries who worked together in a big room typing corporate communications), he heard the sound of productivity that said the business was succeeding. When Boomers worked in teams, they worked by themselves in an office, and they had personal space. But they also wandered and managed. My uncle Jim calls this the walk-and-talk management system. You could walk into someone's office, because everyone had an office, and chat. Boomers' walk-and-talk management style was brought to light in the TV show *Madmen*. It highlighted the fun they had talking, chatting, and entertaining.

What interrupted their way of communicating feedback was the arrival of the personal computer in the office. It led to loss of dialogue. Having dialogue is important to a Boomer; when Ben wants to connect with his team, he wants to use an auditory technology. He likes face-to-face time, and if you have a Boomer on your team, try to get it. Boomers are a wealth of information, but you should plan to spend more than five minutes when learning with them. This dignity in conversation is necessary when giving feedback to, or accepting it from, a Boomer.

Boomer Digital Body Language

Boomers are dignified in their responses and use of digital messaging:

- The goal of their digital body language is to influence.

- They view themselves as big thinkers who build social enterprise, which defines their value to the team as the repository of cultural capital.

- Boomers are feedback disrupters. When thinking through a problem they have received through feedback, Boomers may argue about things that have nothing to do with the topic at hand. This allows them more time to process.

Boomer Giving and Accepting Feedback Triggers

- **Detailed:** Boomers like Ben expect detail. Remember, they give and expect respect in conversation. They can be casual but prefer formality in a feedback situation.

- **Flexible:** Boomers can deal with any situation if they can read the room or see the team's body language. My friend Beverley sits on a number of boards, and she constantly shares the value of going to "meet the people who work in the corporation." She says it is the only way you can *really* learn about a corporation.

- **Give and take:** When they receive feedback, they like it to be respectfully direct. They appreciate being asked detailed questions and anticipate, and look forward to, being pressed for answers.

Language to Avoid When You Give and Accept Feedback to and from a Boomer

- With Ben and his Boomer colleagues, don't use opportunist language. It doesn't work—it only angers. Focusing only on your needs, without identifying how the feedback will help the project or will benefit the person you're communicating with, will fall on deaf ears.

- When accepting feedback, read through all the information. Perhaps even make a few notes and then do further research. Have a plan. Don't respond quickly to Boomers or they will believe you haven't "thought it through."

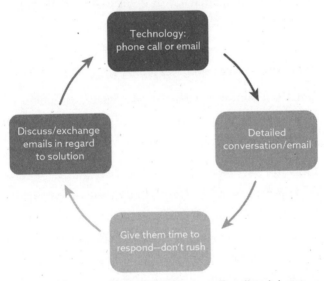

FIGURE 3.2: Suggested Boomer Feedback Loop

Sample Email for Giving Feedback (Can Be Adapted for a Call)

Dear Ben,

I appreciate the work you did on project X. Your knowledge enables us to deliver a quality product on time, and I appreciate your work with the younger team members.

When you have time, I would like to discuss how you are speaking to some members of the team. It's important for the entire team to hear digitally, enabling us to continue to reach our goals for this quarter.

Would it be an imposition if my assistant booked a time for us on Thursday?

Sincerely,

M

Sample Email for Accepting Feedback
(Can Be Adapted for a Call)

Dear Ben,

I appreciate your thoughtful response to how I led the discussion this morning at the team meeting. Your words caused me to rethink my approach. I agree. I may have seemed too casual about a very serious issue. That was not my intention.

I prefer to use humor when addressing the group, and I have found it useful in defusing tension. Team members have told me they appreciate the "dial-it-down" approach when they are stressed, but I can see now that not everyone appreciates this approach. Thank you for bringing this to my attention, and I will work on the tone of my meeting updates.

Sincerely,

M

ADAM THE GEN XER

When Adam was in school, teaching changed, as did the focus on language. Teachers had to go through a more formal process to become educators. They were taught how to use new technologies, classroom management tools, and teaching tools, including flash cards. While in the classroom, students would go to the front or back of the class where a big box containing work cards was located. Students pulled out a card and worked on it while the teacher worked with other groups. Gen Xers worked alone, but together, in the classroom.

Bookmobiles brought books to children, offering a greater variety of books. The Scholastic book sales flyer became a staple in school. Books became the classroom. If your family had money, you got a book—if your family didn't, no books. With one flyer, the haves and have-nots became clearly displayed. Books were still the currency in the classroom, but computers were introduced, and the curious Gen Xers began to explore them at around age 12. Computers, which were a solitary activity without an Internet connection, and the classroom, which encouraged solitary activity yet working together, both framed Gen Xers' digital body language. Computers and TV shaped Gen Xers as the digital sound bite generation, meaning short, blunt, and direct messages. At work, they grew up with personality assessments, including the 360 report and the Myers–Briggs Type Indicator, as feedback tools.

Gen Xer Digital Body Language

Gen X is the "get-down-to-business" generation, and they have a wicked sense of humor:

- Gen Xers view themselves as the workhorses of the organization who will always get the job done. They are the largest cohort today that understands organizational behavior pre-smartphone and post-smartphone, making them the repository of intellectual capital in your workforce.

- They can often be very frank, and they always support their case with facts, occasionally with a visual.

- As holders of your organization's intellectual capital, Gen Xers understand the value of your business and its people, both internally and externally, and how these relationships work with customers.

- The goal of their digital body language is to influence the outcome of work—to solve problems and get stuff done.

- Gen Xers are your feedback bottlenecks. When they stress over feedback, they respond by accepting almost any job from any team member, or from elsewhere in the organization, or by assigning themselves unnecessary tasks (for example, unnecessarily redoing a PowerPoint that didn't look right or re-creating their to-do list on a whiteboard). This slows the team and the project down.

Gen Xer Giving and Accepting Feedback Triggers

- **Macro view:** Gen Xers want to know the plan, and they can fill in the details. When you give them feedback, think of them as you would a general in the army: here is the goal, here's your team, and this is when we need it done.

- **Clarity:** When giving or accepting feedback from Gen Xers, they will relate the feedback back to their 360-review format, career goals, or quarterly sales goals. With Gen X, it's always goals and vision. For example, in an online discussion regarding goals, one participant brought this to life when describing feedback preferences: "All I want is tactics for achieving goals, focus strategies, and improved listening and communication skills, all of which give me building blocks to beneficial change."

- **Direction:** When Gen Xers digitally receive feedback, they skim what they are reading. They want to know that they have achieved the goal, and if they haven't, they begin to think about how they can turn it around. Give them direction to help them succeed.

Language to Avoid When You Give and Accept Feedback to and from a Gen Xer

When giving feedback, be straightforward. Avoid buzzwords such as "socialize." They get too caught up on what "socialize" really means. So instead, just use "share."

When accepting feedback from Gen Xers, be prepared for a workaholic attitude. They expect the job done on time, every time. Gen Xers will talk about timelines, materials, and the end goal. They will not tell you how to do something—they assume you *know* how. When responding to feedback from Gen Xers, keep it as short as possible. Ask the questions you need to ask and make sure they relate to project goals, not yourself (for example, don't say, "I can't work late" or "I don't have time to do this"). Instead, relate your statements back to the project or ask them to help you prioritize your time.

Sample Email for Giving Feedback

Hi Adam,

I wanted to share an update with you on your progress as the new client manager.

As you can see, you are off to a great start, and the key indicators are:

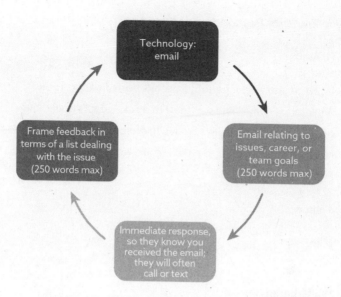

FIGURE 3.3: Suggested Gen Xer Feedback Loop

- We now have 100% client participation. *Remember*, I still need the report for this survey.

- Your presentation today went well. However, you need to engage the clients more with their data. For example, ask them questions before you give them an answer.

I've been receiving thoughtful feedback from your team on your presentation and look forward to speaking with you about this more.

Please choose a date from the options on my calendar link below. We will need 30 minutes, and I want this completed by next Friday [insert date].

Have a great weekend,

M

Sample Email for Responding to Feedback

Hi Adam,

I appreciate your thoughts on my performance today. I think this is something we need to discuss. Let's book time on the calendar—see link below. To enable this to be a solid learning for both of us, please ensure we meet before next Friday.

Thanks,

Mary

Trish the Millennial

At the time Trish and other Millennials began school, a lot of social change was taking place. Divorce was becoming more common, more mothers were working full time, and teaching protocols were changing from grade shaming to positive affirmation. This trend also included viewing education as a business, which meant education was looking at efficiencies in teaching. Grouping desks together and working on team projects became the norm. Books and flash cards were eventually replaced with the Internet and online games.

Millennials were the first generation to have a TV and a computer in the family room, enabling them to easily begin multitasking with technology. This latchkey generation lived in a constant feedback loop. Their parents—because both were working or one was living in another household—spoke with them on the phone more, and eventually through other communication technology. This built a much stronger bond, as frequent feedback does. Parenting trends of the time reflected teaching trends: parents didn't criticize, and they worked to ensure their kids were confident in their abilities. Feedback was framed as a suggestion, not a declarative statement.

Millennial Digital Body Language

Millennials are the great charmers of any workforce, and their confidence can often be infectious:

- In terms of digital body language, Millennials are very appealing in their response and their digital messaging. This makes them the repository of communication capital. They understand how to use digital body language to motivate.

- The goal of their digital body language is to influence the group. They are motivated by group brainstorming, ideas, and action.

- They view themselves as the Picassos of an organization. They work through design, and creativity rules their digital body language.

- Millennials are the feedback fidgets. When unclear on feedback, they go to social media. They will mute a conference call to work on other projects or flip through their messages while you speak with them. They fidget, look at their phone, and tend to avoid eye contact.

Millennial Giving and Accepting Feedback Triggers

- **How:** Provide detailed instructions. This is the generation that worked in groups, and that means everything must be clear and defined, enabling each member to get his or her job done.

- **Use logic:** This generation doesn't accept feedback if they don't see the reason for the task. They will question it. To avoid this back and forth, outline the logic quickly and then provide the supporting data.

Language to Avoid When You Give and Accept Feedback
to and from a Millennial

- **Narrow in scope:** Don't use language that may be considered "off-humor." According to the Pew Research Center, "Millennials have brought more racial and ethnic diversity to American society, they appreciate all members of the team, and expect equality for all."[5]

- **Avoid too much detail:** This generation multitasks and flicks through emails. If possible, create an overview (for example, a "project overview") and insert a link to this overview in your email. Then give them direction about next steps.

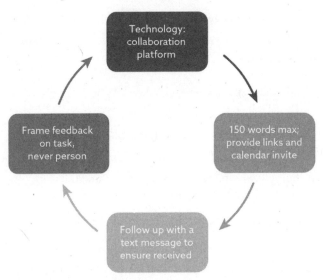

FIGURE 3.4: Suggested Millennial Feedback Loop

Example of Giving Feedback (Given in
Collaboration Platform Teams)

Trish, thanks for the report. I'll connect with Don. Let's get it drafted this week. We will need to do more research.

Please be the lead on this, socialize it, and then you and I should chat on Tuesday. Does 9 a.m. work? If not, please book another time on Tuesday.

Thanks, ☺

Example of Accepting Feedback (Sent as a Text)

Trish, I appreciate the feedback. Let's have a call today to discuss your ideas. Does 4:30 work? If not, good tomorrow morning.

Tyler the Gen Zer

Tyler entered a school that was already digital. Homework and other assignments were posted on technology like Google Classroom. Children were familiar with social media and used it to learn from each other. Desk groupings were not only the norm in the classroom, they became virtual groupings through Facebook chat groups. Online, students played with toys that were connected to the web, including the short-lived trend of Webkins, little toys that had a code and stayed alive based on how often students connected to the Internet. Gen Zers understand that technology makes them visible.

More than any other generation since the Greatest Generation (pre-Boomers), clearly defined rules and policies, as well as clear feedback, help Gen Zers succeed. They are also visual, and they have become accustomed to using emojis and texting with their parents and grandparents. To Gen Zers, Facebook and Twitter are old-fashioned. Their feedback tools are short, quick videos or a FaceTime video chat. They like to see the person who is delivering feedback to them.

Other than the increased use of technology, parenting trends and teaching trends changed only slightly to accommodate the stress and pressure of the recession and the changing morals of the United States. However, parents stopped framing feedback as a question and started to go back to the declarative style, as did teachers. When students are looking at multiple screens, long answers don't sink in; therefore, feedback is best when it is short, to the point, and followed up with a video call or a phone call.

Gen Zer Digital Body Language

Gen Z is the logical, inventive, and capable generation. Gen Zers take comfort in security and rules:

- In terms of digital body language, Gen Zers are clipped communicators. They are direct and to the point.

- Gen Zers are the repository of your digital capital. They know how to organize and drive digitally.

- The goal of their digital body language is to succeed and then accomplish change.

- They view themselves as change makers, like the people whose tools they have been using their entire lives (for example, Steve Jobs and Mark Zuckerberg).

- Gen Zers are feedback fixated. You can tell Gen Zers are not receiving the feedback and accolades they need when they demand a lot of time and attention. This generation needs daily feedback on their performance.

Gen Zer Giving and Accepting Feedback Triggers

- **Be consistent:** Most Gen Zers don't adapt well to sudden change. Therefore, when giving them feedback or accepting feedback from them, ensure you stay on message. Don't throw them a curve ball. This generation was brought up on algorithms, "likes," logic, and clear feedback, not emotionally charged discussions that they often consider rants.

- **You can be top down:** This generation likes the comfort of a hierarchy and a clear and consistent path of respectful feedback. They have seen how feedback posted online can derail a conversation.

Language to Avoid When You Give and Accept Feedback to and from a Gen Zer

- **Ambiguity:** This generation doesn't deal well with uncertainty.

- **Conflict:** This generation can hold their own in an argument, but they dislike conflict because they've seen too much of it.

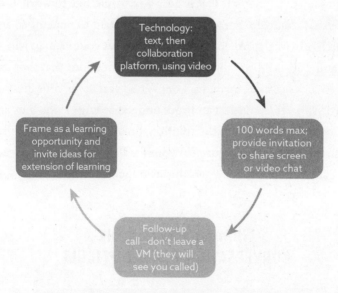

FIGURE 3.5: Suggested Gen Zer Feedback Loop

Example of Giving Feedback (Sent as a Message in Teams or a Direct Message)

> The abstract is in good shape. Your conclusion needs to be more robust. Attached are a few examples of what I want to see. Need to chat?

Example of Accepting Feedback

> Great work—you made me think—I love that. Let's brainstorm—free to chat?

━►

Why is it important to understand this information for each of these generations? Because shifting how you provide and receive feedback enables you to motivate your entire team. Many people in my speaking audiences have challenged me on this, saying that others should learn to adapt to them. If that is how you would like to work, then absolutely, please do. For a leader, it is important to remember, and research proves, that when you are trying to get your team to win, as Jose and Tony said, you have to give them directions that they can understand, see value in, and act on. When you tailor your messaging, you show them respect and your understanding of who they are.

You can now move to the solution, breaking the barrier of providing the right body language in your feedback and avoiding feedback generational stress triggers during difficult conversations.[6]

WHAT TO DO WHEN THE CONVERSATION TURNS DIFFICULT

For some of us, the four words "we need to talk" are anxiety-inducing. Don't believe me? Try saying them to someone you love or work with and watch the reaction on his or her face. Or text these words to a friend and wait for the response. I tried it with my daughter—even the queen of cool herself was anxious. Difficult conversations are like vegetables: you may not like them, but you need them to be healthy. When discussing leadership, participants in my survey who worked at the Greenheck Fan Corporation said they felt difficult conversations were not only the hardest to hear but also one of the most challenging aspects of being a leader, no matter their generation.[7]

As the quote from a Gen X leader demonstrates:

> I learned that feedback can be challenging to receive for all of us and that it's important to transition into viewing feedback as a learning opportunity in order to better absorb it and improve. I've been working on being more receptive to feedback by defusing my stress prior to entering the feedback session. This way I'm more receptive.

Organizations also face a particularly interesting challenge in having difficult conversations with Millennials and Gen Zers, although for different reasons (as discussed later in the chapter). In school, teachers work hard not to fail their students because the focus is on their students' success. But in my opinion, we need to build more failure into our education system to allow students to learn how to have difficult conversations.

When I counsel executives, I suggest they train their teams to have difficult conversations. Two of the great trainers, in my opinion, are Dr. Sheila Heen and Dr. Douglas Stone. Their books *Thanks for the Feedback* and *Difficult Conversations* are immense resources, and I have recommended them to all my clients. They are no-nonsense scientists who explain, in simple terms, why these conversations must be had and how to have them.

All experts agree: great communicators understand how to identify distress, bring people out of it, and move forward with difficult conversations. Dale Carnegie, who wrote the seminal book *How to Win Friends and Influence People,* claims that if you can deliver difficult news well, you will be more successful in any job you choose. Another way to prepare yourself for having a difficult conversation is by reviewing the Generational Anchoring Benchmarks.

GENERATIONAL ANCHORING BENCHMARKS: DEALING WITH DIFFICULT CONVERSATIONS

TABLE 3.1: **Generational Anchoring Benchmarks: Difficult Conversations (DCs)**

	Experience with DCs	Digital Body Language for DCs	Stress Cues in Sentence Patterning	Quick Fixes
Boomers	Learned from middle management; excellent with DCs	Be very direct	"You are not OK"	Call them, listen to them, and then state your case; do not get drawn off track with their chatter—keep it focused
Gen Xers	Did not learn DC from middle management	Present a request	"I don't know"	Frame your feedback in terms of benefits and obstacles; outline the benefits as they relate to them and the company; and then point out what some of the obstacles are going to be

	Experience with DCs	Digital Body Language for DCs	Stress Cues in Sentence Patterning	Quick Fixes
Millennials	Didn't have a lot of opportunity to have DCs	Be nurturing	"I'm OK, but you are not"	Provide clarity and proof; they will again blame you, but if they see the proof, they will calm down
Gen Zers	Doesn't mind DCs at all—just add a dash of humor	Be nurturing	"You are wrong"	They also need clarity and digital proof; they, too, need proof to calm down.

- **Boomers** grew up with middle management. They were hauled on the carpet when they screwed up and were allowed to learn on the job. They learned the value of difficult conversations and to appreciate a logical argument.

- **Gen Xers** didn't have middle management. They were the generation that was constantly told to do more with less. Screwing up meant they were fired. Difficult conversations were held infrequently or during an exit interview. The Jack Welch style of management adopted by many Fortune 500 companies caused Gen Xers to avoid difficult conversations, persevere, and get the job done—no matter what. They knew if they didn't, they could lose their jobs. In the Welch system, the bottom percentile of performers was fired annually.

- **Millennials** never had difficult conversations. Rather, they had coaching conversations. Our school system stopped failing students, which stifled competitiveness, so the focus became self-esteem. While Millennials turned out to be good human interactors, we failed them because we didn't give them the opportunity to fail and learn. Now they need to be taught the value of a difficult conversation and how to have one.

- **Gen Zers** don't mind difficult conversations at all, but when they do have them, they prefer them with a touch of humor. Because this generation has grown up with death, destruction, and guns in the classroom, they will not shy away from a difficult conversation, but it is best to prepare them for it. They will also let you know what is on their minds. Since they have developed with the give-and-take of the Internet, they don't understand boundaries or decorum—they just talk. In your onboarding, ensure that you provide Gen Zers with cultural guidelines on how to have difficult conversations. When having a difficult conversation, let them move around. Don't force them to sit and stare at you while you talk to them.

Digital Body Language for a Difficult Conversation

When you're having difficult conversations with your team or requesting something from them, members from each generation will respond differently. Use the following formulas and you'll receive the best results:

- **Boomers:** Be very direct.

- **Gen Xers:** Present a request.

- **Millennials and Gen Zers:** Be nurturing.

For each of these formulas, use this sequence of reflective listening skills:

1. Encourage employees to talk about their perception of how they understand an area of improvement.

2. Ask employees to define a problem as it relates to their understanding of the organization's goals.

3. Ask employees to define, through these changes, their role within the organization.

4. Outline your perception of their behavior.

5. Allow them time to process this.

6. Present your next steps.

7. Ask them for feedback.

8. Create a resolution.

Digital body language can help us identify stress and reduce fear, enabling us to conduct a difficult conversation, and each generation has some pretty telltale signs. For example:

- **Boomers** use sentence patterning that directly blames you for the problem, such as "you are not okay."

- **Gen Xers** use sentence patterning that is defensive, such as "I don't know" or "How would I know?"

- **Millennials** use sentence patterning that absolves them of blame but blames you, such as "I'm okay, but you are not."

- **Gen Zers** either don't respond at all or use a direct response, such as "you are wrong."

There are also quick fixes to reduce this stress and get the difficult feedback on track for each generation, such as:

- **Boomers** need direct feedback: "This is what I need you to do because then we're going to get this result, and this result is going to benefit your pension." This approach also works very well for Gen Zers. Call them, listen to them, and then state your case. Do not get drawn off track with their chatter—keep it focused.

- **Gen Xers** do not trust leadership; they trust their team, so they always fear the worst from leaders. Therefore, you need to be very logical in how you construct your feedback to help them get the job done. Frame your feedback in terms of benefits and obstacles. Outline the benefits as they relate to them and the company; then point out what some of the obstacles are going to be.

- **Millennials and Gen Zers** have something in common— they want clarity. When you are trying to reduce their stress, ensure that the focus is not on them but on the action and the action's results. Have proof. They will again blame you, but if they see the proof, they will calm down.

With members of all generations, when you have difficult news, don't hedge about it. Boomers will discount you. Gen Xers will spend more time worrying and rethinking what they did, focusing on fallback plans rather than tasks. Millennials and Gen Zers will just check things with their friends, their contacts, and online, and if you lie or try to hide things, they will shut down, or worse, they will leave. These generations can handle the truth. They just require a customized approach.

To understand why we have digital misunderstandings, we have identified each generation's digital body language. This drives your excellence as a digital communicator. Feedback, whether positive or negative, is what propels us. But what binds us together is culture. To understand how to create a great culture, you need to leverage your knowledge of generational culture triggers.

CHAPTER FOUR

STEP 4:
IDENTIFY GENERATIONAL
TRIGGERS

Prior to the COVID-19 crisis, relatively few people had heard of my work, which makes sense. The crisis changed the way we work together, and it changed the minds of people who did not believe generational soft skills had anything to do with their work culture, particularly my clients in the armed forces. But they came around once they saw the data and saw themselves and their teams in the data.

As a bit of context, companies previously preferred to believe researchers like the brilliant Dr. Jennifer Deal. In her influential book *Retiring the Generation Gap: How Employees Young & Old Can Find Common Ground*, she argues there are only a few basic differences between generations and members of all generations want the same thing. Many CEOs and academic institutions agreed with her at the time, because, as one executive told me, "it is much easier to agree."

I concur with Dr. Deal on one point: the generation gap is based on misunderstanding and miscommunication. As she states, "The so-called generation gap is, in large part, the result of miscommunication and misunderstanding, fueled by common insecurities and the desire for clout."[1] Writing pre-smartphone, Dr. Deal couldn't have imagined the extent to which technology would change communication and amplify these "common insecurities." The COVID pandemic proved just how misunderstandings and insecurities can be amplified when companies tried to move to a digital culture overnight. If you don't know your team's digital cultural triggers, you cannot know your team.

A digital culture that doesn't exist naturally alongside a team's face-to-face culture presents roadblocks in the everyday aspects of work. This then leads to team misunderstandings, which leads to a culture that is not performing at its highest possible level.

Culture is a set of specific standards that dictate how each team member behaves at work. For team members, no matter what their role, culture guides how work is done—what is right and what is wrong. A workplace culture is usually set by the CEO. Like ice cream on a hot day, it slowly melts down into the organization and influences every decision people make. But how does culture make itself felt in a digital world? During the COVID pandemic, many companies struggled to digitally adapt their culture. But few team members had ever given much thought to their teams' digital cultures. This added to the stress brought on by social distancing. People felt disconnected and alone. Connecting digitally didn't feel human. During the COVID crisis, I had clients and former teaching colleagues asking me questions about how to create digital culture for both a classroom and a workplace.

One former colleague, an "older" professor, suddenly stopped teaching when all of his school's classes were forced to go online. The professor had no idea how to use the technology because he had never used it before. The tech team couldn't go to his house to help him because everyone was practicing social distancing. The school's culture had always allowed tenured professors to teach as they preferred to. For example, professors were never required to train to use a learning management system (LMS). During COVID, the school's culture failed the students.

In the corporate world, not having a digital culture caused a costly loss of productivity for a firm of over 7,000 people. The CEO's strong belief in a face-to-face culture led to a financial disaster. No matter how many times his team had pleaded with him to support telecommunicating, he would say, "No," and state, "We are a face-to-face team: we always have been, and always will be." Even at the beginning of the COVID pandemic, he maintained this position, but he was forced to rethink it. The governor of his state ordered everyone, except essential services, to work from home. I was called because one of the C-level team members had heard me speak before, and she thought I might have some suggestions. I did. I suggested she take the company's digital cultural pulse.

HOW TO TAKE YOUR COMPANY'S
DIGITAL CULTURAL PULSE

Each generation uses technology differently based on the habits they have acquired. We identified these in the previous chapters as generational anchoring benchmarks (GABs). Conflicting GABs result in a digital cultural clash and unintentional stress triggers. They slow us down, but the solution is as simple as taking your pulse.

When you take your pulse, you put your fingers on your wrist and count the beats you feel over 15 seconds. You then multiply this number by four to find out how many times your heart beats per minute. Your team's digital cultural pulse is just as simple to take. You can estimate the age ranges of your team members by using the generational guide in this book. For example, in the year 2020, if you estimate someone is between 61 and 75, he or she would be a Boomer. Next, if you think someone is under 60 but older than 40, he or she is a Gen Xer. A team member under 40 and over 20 is a Millennial, and a team member under 20 is a Gen Zer.

When I take a client's digital cultural pulse, the team leaders involved ask HR for the *approximate* age of the largest and second largest age groups in their teams. (Other team leaders have just known this information and told me.) Once you know the first and second largest generations in your teams, meet and share the teams' cultural descriptions and suggest "fixes" accordingly (which we will discuss throughout this chapter). What I have found during this digital culture discussion is that teams either use the solutions suggested in this chapter or come up with new ones. All the solutions limit the variance in communication between the generations.

Dr. Edward Deming, the father of modern productivity, believed that if you reduce the variance in a product, you increase the efficiency of that product. Your product as a team is *communication*. Your job is to efficiently and effectively communicate and produce, which is what all salaries and bonuses are based on. When you reduce the variance in communication, you create more clarity and you can produce more. Understanding your team's digital pulse reduces variance in communication and increases your productivity. At least it did for Microsoft, Walmart, and Greenheck, all global corporations, with which I have worked, that want to support the individuals on their teams in every way possible, lifting their productivity to drive results and profits.

DEFINING DIGITAL CULTURE

In order to move into the next phase of the book, where we measure the digital pulse of a team, we need a working definition of culture.

For our purposes, let us describe **culture** as *a set of norms or habits that define a group and enable it to thrive*. In the case of **workplace culture**, culture is thought to be *how the group acts as a collective to accomplish its goals*. To enable you to take your team's digital pulse, here are six aspects that will guide the discussion:

- Routine

- Rules

- Creativity

- Decision making

- Motivators

- Cultural stress triggers

Digital Cultural Pulse: Boomers

Routine

Ben is a great preparer, like all Boomers, who, according to the Pew Research Center, make up 25 percent of most teams.[2] As discussed in Chapter 3, in terms of work paradigms, Boomers are the holders of cultural capital, more so than any other generation. Their skill set as team members is underpinned by their knowledge of the cultural development of a business and what makes it tick. A Boomer team culture trades in having conversations and connecting. Boomers prefer to directly hear how tasks and projects are progressing. They like to be deliberate in their work and will not be rushed. Their strength as team members is in building teams and consensus. For example, when I interviewed a Boomer union leader, he shared an example of how he used a jacket to build a culture of acceptance in a specific town. The union was hoping to get more people to not only accept the idea of a union at one of the largest employers in town but to join the union as well. The union leader felt that if his members wore union-branded jackets around town, people might see how many members the union had and be less afraid to join. The jacket was a symbol of strength in numbers, and it proved that joining a union was an acceptable social norm. He used the jacket as a symbol to build a culture in the same way sports teams do when their fans wear the teams' shirts on game day.

Rules

Boomers view meetings as a way to exchange information as a group. For this reason, they particularly like the formality of status meetings. However, when participants talk too much, fail to stick to the agenda, or ignore the person who has the floor, Boomers become upset because they feel as if the group's time is being wasted.

Creativity

Boomers focus on culture as the anchor for their creativity. When offered a structured meeting and time to think, they do their best work. They create based on the organization's mission. Their preference is to create together in a room, go away and think, and come back together as a team for consensus. They don't need reminders for meetings, but they do appreciate them. They use technology to identify, schedule, and set expectations for the meeting. They prefer the comfort of *Robert's Rules of Order*—the well-known manual that explains methods to run a board meeting or any meeting requiring motions and voting—to create a team meeting structure and then stick to it.

Decision Making

Boomers use consensus building in committees to move a project forward. They will dial into a meeting if they cannot attend in person. Email is their technology preference. They are reluctant to embrace video.

Motivators

When beginning a project, Boomers appreciate black-and-white guidelines on meeting and reporting structures. When using video calling, give them clear instructions on how to sign in and steps to take if the technology is not working, such as calling tech support. When meeting through technology, at the top of the call, identify who will be speaking and their responsibilities for the project. Introduce online and informal opportunities to connect and find similarities outside of social media. Create opportunities to mentor team members who want to grow their skills and move ahead in the organization.

Cultural Stress Trigger: Legacy Anxiety

Boomers grew up with global anxiety and a desire to make a difference with their lives. Indications that they are experiencing cultural stress include talking about how engaged they are with the job, how loyal they are, what they are doing to build the company, and what, in their opinion, is wrong. If a project is going awry and Boomer leaders are struggling, you will notice that they will send emails that talk about how, in their experience, this has never happened before. In those emails, they will blame teams for hurting productivity and even become angry at others because their legacies are being affected. If you manage Boomers, use this structure as a guide to de-escalating their stress and solve their stress triggers:

- List their accomplishments and the accomplishments of the team; this will recognize their legacy.

- Talk to them to help define the next steps in resolving the problem.

Digital Cultural Pulse: Gen Xers

Routine

Adam, our Gen Xer, is a member of the generation most determined to succeed. Gen Xers make up 35 percent of most workforces.[3] As seen in Chapter 3, in terms of work paradigms, they are the holders of intellectual capital, more so than any other generation. Their skill as team members is building strategies and tactics that can move the organization through change. A Gen Xer team culture trades in the currency of time and goals. Gen Xers are energized by seeing how goals are reached and projects are advancing. Gen Xers are conscientious and superb tacticians—core strengths they bring to the team.

Rules

Gen Xers view meetings as an opportunity to get things done. They organize and direct the meetings. Since they are less immersed in technology than some other generations, they prefer face-to-face meetings, as compared to virtual ones, during which they animatedly present ideas, discuss them, and then take action. When Gen Xers have no clear sense that a meeting will be productive, they withdraw from it. Signs of this withdrawal include looking up and away from the speaker or focusing on their computers or notebooks.

To bring them out of this stress, one hour or so before the start of the meeting, send a meeting check-in. A meeting check-in email, sent to the group before a meeting, serves as a gentle reminder that the meeting is happening, who is responsible for bringing what to the meeting, who is attending, and who will be absent.

Once the meeting starts, review the check-in and ensure that all of the participants are on the same page. Have all the team members who need to update the team give a short spoken project status update. This is also a great way to start a meeting with Gen Zers. It is a quick, simple method that picks up where the last meeting ended, facilitates project collaboration, and closes any gaps. A brief example of a meeting check-in is as follows:

Meeting Absences

Don has his surgery tomorrow—and we are all thinking good thoughts—Rhonda has a crazy full day with her family. Neither is able to attend.

Project Updates

Company A Cohort #5: Mohammad Reporting

Company A #5 midterm: done

- Midterm results to client by Sept. 1

- Client only has a week to review

- Results being compiled, and Rhonda indicated she will forward

- Don: don't worry about editing

Company B: Mark Is Calling Participants This Week

- Midterm: done

- Status call, re: results completed

- Mark will call all participants this week to keep them on their game—this is a really important cohort as we need to get deeper with client

New Contracts: Randy

Randy will send Tracy copies of the signed contracts, which will be completed on the following dates:

- Company X: August 4
- Company Y: August 9
- Company Z: August 24

Creativity

Gen Xers create alone, person to machine. Gen Xers use technology to help them frame their solution for presentation. A creative solution for them is one that builds the relationship between external clients and internal team members. They like to see how people are cocreating on their team, as it shows productive creativity. They like to see multiple uploads of one PowerPoint presentation, as it allows them to go back and see the changes that have been made. The deep desire to keep all drafts satisfies Gen Xers' conscientious workplace attitude, defined as proving that work has been done and that people have "earned" their pay.

Decision Making

Gen Xers make decisions based on the purpose of the project. They think in terms of gray and weigh all the options. The question "What if?" plagues them, and they often think about it far too late into the night. That is why a shared drive, like Google Drive, enables them to go back and see previous editions of a document, helping them to create the next version. They take great pains to make decisions based on the overall goals of the project and will stand by them. Collaboration software allows Gen Xers to see how others are making decisions and moving a project forward. For this reason, when you require a decision from Gen Xers, enable them to see the facts and provide access to them any time of the day.

Motivators

Gen Xers are like the famous actress Greta Garbo—at times they just want to be "alone." They value their alone time and appreciate physical spaces that can give that to them. Gen Xers became accustomed to technology at work through digital access, meaning the Internet, and the ability to access files online, but also through programs such as PowerPoint and Word. Some Gen Xers even remember when data were stored on discs. The Internet was an individual experience, as were work and training. Managers managed you, and you managed your tasks. In regard to technology, this means their great motivator is time to themselves in the day, during which they can get through their emails or draft a PowerPoint. They appreciate the opportunity to shut the door and work without notifications or interruptions. The "time to stand" Apple Watch app was made for this group. They will become immersed in their technology and sit for hours, working in front of a screen.

Cultural Stress Trigger: Time

Gen Xers have an obsession with time. They always feel they never have enough of it. When people are late for a meeting, they are almost grateful, as it gives them time to answer an email, but they are also resentful, as they know they will be late for their next meeting, and the next one, and so on. An indication that they are experiencing cultural stress is when they get frustrated with people who are not on the same wavelength. They will criticize others for not "being on the same page." This occurs when Gen Xers do not understand how each tactic fits into the big picture. If you manage Gen Xers, de-escalate their stress by using this sentence patterning:

- Show them exactly what is happening in a project or other deliverable that they are accountable for.

- Use a visual.

- Outline the big picture and show them you know what the current obstacles are and what future obstacles might arise.

- Ask them, "How do you *see* a particular strategy working, and what roadblocks might impact the strategy?" Another example is asking them what roadblock they are *picturing* with this strategy.

Digital Cultural Pulse: Millennials

Routine

Trish is part of the great adaptor generation. Millennials make up 38 percent of the workforce.[4] As mentioned in Chapter 3, in terms of work paradigms, they are the holders of communication capital, more so than any other generation. A Millennial team culture trades in the currency of sharing and opinions. They value online relationships and time away from work. They will work at odd hours to accommodate their varying outside interests, but technology facilitates this very well. They are not the generation to be stuck behind a desk. Millennials very capably connect and work with one another, both online and offline. Another one of their strengths is that they are consummate socializers who drive change.

Rules

Millennials appreciate a calendar that guides their days and highlights their meetings. Millennials view meetings as an opportunity to collaborate and will consider a meeting a waste of time if the team doesn't share and collaborate in a meaningful way during it. A wasted meeting for Millennial teams is one in which they do not have the opportunity to collaborate and share. They like to read items and discuss them in the meeting. Their goal in a meeting is to meaningfully contribute. Their highest level of participation occurs in intelligent meetings, defined as meetings driven by technology.

This generation makes good use of online calendars. Be sure to send Millennials reminders to prepare for a meeting. They value reminders, which can be scheduled in most office technologies (for example, Outlook, Apple, and Gmail calendars). As we will learn in the chapter on collaborative meetings (Chapter 5), on average, Millennials attend 10 meetings a week, and anything that can be done to help them participate in a meeting more fully will generate higher productivity.

Creativity

Millennials create with each other through a machine. Texting is the new watercooler chat. They are motivated to create by an action that needs to be taken or a problem that needs to be solved. They need clear direction but do not limit their use of social media—it is how they communicate and test their theories.

Decision Making

Millennials use social media to make decisions. They were taught to share, and technology assists them in making informed decisions. Incorporate social media links, including ones to YouTube, into your creative collaboration. Millennials use social media to find and make comparisons. Let them. In John Adams's time as the second president of the United States, people used information from a multitude of local, personal newspapers to make their decisions. Today, we would call these blogposts and podcasts.

Motivators

Millennials respond to links, videos, sharing, social media, and team comparisons. Millennials love multitasking, which means watching one thing, listening to another, and creating yet another. Make use of Slack and Microsoft Teams to enable their multitasking. Embrace the fact that this group will multitask, which means they will text or email in meetings. This group did their homework, watched Netflix, and sent texts to friends all within a few quick swipes of their fingers.

To socialize ideas in meetings, use Slack messaging or Microsoft Teams—such programs give everyone in the meeting a view of how the team is reacting to the meeting. Millennials work to get an *A* and want the rubric to measure their success. Give them the structure that nurtures engagement.

Cultural Stress Triggers: Development

Millennials have been "developed" or trained for the next big thing their entire lives. Some parents started SAT training for their Millennial children years before they were eligible to take the test. If you do not provide your Millennials with professional development opportunities, they will get stressed and disengage. Development is their benchmark that says you are invested in them and that you want them to move forward and succeed.

An indication that they are experiencing cultural stress is that they tune out. They look right at you but seem to look through you. You can see they are not listening, but they smile and nod. They tell you how frustrated they are with people who do not believe in them, and they list all of their talents in detail. Often, they will try to hold you hostage with this behavior, as they know they are a valued commodity. If you manage Millennials, de-escalate their stress by using this sentence patterning:

- Tell them their value. Praise their contribution.

- Show them how you plan to help them develop professionally. Demonstrate for them a means to an end.

Digital Cultural Pulse: Gen Zers

Routine

Tyler is part of the doer generation. More than any other generation since the Great Depression, this generation will make change happen. If you haven't read or heard about it, Gen Zers are holding Boomer leaders accountable with their "OK Boomer" campaign.

It all started with Boomers dismissing Gen Zers' call for change, and matters soon escalated. Gen Z is the first generation to get even small changes considered in gun laws, most likely because, of all the generations, they have been the most affected by gun violence. They have no issue with causing conflict on a team; they prefer not to, but they will. As of today, Gen Zers make up 5 percent of most teams,[5] but they are quickly entering the workforce. As explored in Chapter 3, in terms of work paradigms, they are the holders of technological capital, more so than any other generation. They almost instinctively know the right application to use to connect with the right people for the right outcomes.

Rules

This generation meets through visual technology, auditory technology, and memes. Google takes too long, and now YouTube is the fastest growing search engine for Gen Zers, who watch videos instead of spending time on other media. When they meet, they do so digitally, in the cloud and "face to face." Apple's FaceTime app enables video calling at a touch of a button, and most other collaboration platforms also have this feature. When required to attend meetings, they always have their phones with them. They often write notes, but they are also the people called on at work, and at home, to fix all the technology bugs or, during meetings, to introduce their teams to the next big thing.

Creativity

Gen Zers communicate and create on the cloud as a team. They used it in school, working on projects on the cloud. They don't know anything but the cloud. To them, creativity is always a group activity: you share what you like or don't like; you brainstorm; you write. It was how they were educated—as a team, not as an individual.

Decision Making

Gen Zers are the most patient of all team members and are terrific mentors because they have had to teach each other throughout their school lives. They create groups to share and make decisions. These groups often lock out other people. For example, students use Facebook groups to set up events for events like frosh week, which is the start of university life for many college freshmen, instead of using the technology the university wants them to use. The events go smoothly, and technology allows for group decision making.

Motivators

Gen Z team culture trades in the currency of technology and speed. Their currency is online. They can manage multiple tasks with ease. Their strength is in their ability to connect with technology and use it to get the job done quickly and efficiently. They are the go-getters who drive change. Gen Zers grew up in the age of short videos, so they watch and hear. Do not expect Gen Zers to read in the traditional sense. They will read a book while listening to the audiobook version as a way to speed up the narration and meet their mental processing needs. Enable them to process information in nontraditional formats.

Cultural Stress Triggers: Deflection

This amiable, intelligent generation can deflect with ease. When they don't understand or can't make sense of something, Gen Zers change the topic. An indication that they are experiencing cultural stress is that they deflect. When people talk in "long form," which means long and detailed explanations, they tend to shut down, as they have never had the experience of just listening. Indications that they are trying to deflect include fidgeting, looking away or down, and even moving away from you. If you manage Gen Zers, de-escalate their stress by using this sentence patterning:

- Briefly focus on the task or behavior you are discussing and then outline the means to an end.

- Give them time to absorb what you said and then ask them their understanding of what you said.

If you are in a situation in which you can only give email feedback to reduce cultural stress, try the following for each generation:

- **Boomers:** Use long and detailed emails or reports.

- **Gen Xers:** Create a list or a visual that they can look at and understand when speaking.

- **Millennials:** Create a checklist they can prepare before they meet with you. Demonstrate they have a responsibility in this conversation. Ensure the checklist is sent to you beforehand.

- **Gen Zers:** Give them bulleted points. Be clear and link all of the points.

IS YOUR CULTURE WORKING?

Historically, companies have treated workers simply as a means to an end. Workers could be replaced easily and quickly. Any leader who continues to hold this belief is doomed by the new realities of the way people think about work. As a leader, you have to recognize that your competitive edge lies in your team's ability to collaborate and converse, and that means shifting your digital body language to meet the needs of your team.

But how do you know if a team culture needs to be repaired? Are you reaching your goals? Are there delays in delivery? Are there instances of insubordination, defined as not listening to a leader, occurring on a daily, weekly, or monthly basis? As Jabo Floyd, who ignited my interest in the topic of communication and generations, once told me, people sometimes just know when a team's culture needs to change. Sometimes there is nothing like just being on the floor, meeting with the people, and watching their faces as they work. You get it—you know if your culture is working. As history proves, culture and motivation are tied together.

Good science is based on theory that has been proved true time and time again; the science of a productive culture is no exception. Elton Mayo's work rarely achieved consensus in academic circles, which, in my opinion, is a sign of greatness. (If you haven't read about the Hawthorne effect, it's worth googling.) His major discovery was that to be a productive civilization or have an innovative workplace, you have to pay attention to your people. If you do that, even by saying hello and asking about a person's family, people will be more productive. Mayo was the father of productivity measures, influencing Edward Deming, the father of modern productivity measurements. Dr. Deming himself observed, "People are part of the system; they need help . . . Many people think of machinery and data processing when I mention system. Few of them know that recruitment, training, supervision, and aids to production workers are part of the system."[6]

Chester Barnard, whose work is discussed in Chapter 2, created work teams. Students are now educated and work in teams. Barnard established the theory that by working together, teams could solve problems faster and make a product better. The idea was not to manage each other, go to meetings, or answer emails (at that time it was memos) but rather to solve problems. Kurt Lewin said that cultural behavior is a function of people and the environment. A crappy environment equals crappy work. Peter Drucker ties it all together by saying that not only should you care about the environment people are working in, but it will serve you well to see them, acknowledge them, and even speak to them.

To reduce cultural stress in your organization, my advice is to create digital cultural norms that will help team members manage up and down. Here are a few suggestions my clients have put into place with their teams and clients.

The Rules of Texting

Understand and define who you are texting and what his or her relationship is with technology and then operate with the following in mind:

- **Boomers** need full explanations. Don't just send them a bunch of emojis—they will think you have gone mad!

- **Gen Xers** like PowerPoints and charts with brief text explanations.

- **Millennials** adore emojis.

- **Gen Zers** prefer Snapchat and video.

The Rules of Emailing Good and Bad News

You must keep in mind how each generation was introduced to work:

- **Boomers** are very formal. They prefer an email in the form of a letter (for example, starting with "Dear [recipient's name],"). They like well-written correspondence. Whether relaying bad or good news, be clear, logical, and avoid casual conversation at all costs.

- **Gen Xers** appreciate brevity and PowerPoint decks. Use charts and to-do lists with calendar invitations and follow up with a deck and clear guidelines. When conveying good news, simply state your point. If conveying bad news, be direct. If it is the fault of the person you are contacting, state that and then suggest next steps. If it's your fault, own it and then suggest next steps.

- **Millennials** like everything to be in black and white. Send an email invitation and provide an agenda with supporting links. Tell them only what they need to know. When delivering bad news, frame it as a learning opportunity and allow time for a conversation. When you provide them with good news, they will accept it, and you should anticipate that they will digitally share it.

- **Gen Zers** do not email, so you must teach them how. When providing them with bad or good news, you should be brief; ask for feedback, such as, "How does that make you feel?"; and address what you see as next steps. With Gen Zers, you have to pull them into a conversation. Unlike Millennials and their willingness to chat, this generation wants to learn and move on.

VIRTUAL PROJECT TEAMS

Questions we run up against in the world of virtual project teams include "What happens if we don't know someone's age and cannot establish their generation?" and "How can a leader who is taking over a failing virtual team fix the situation?"

For virtual project teams, I always recommend you use your digital emotional intelligence (DEQ). As a reminder, DEQ, mentioned in the Introduction, is your ability to recognize patterns in the messages you receive, enabling you to understand what people are saying to you and predict how people are going to engage with you. It empowers you to solve problems quickly and effectively. DEQ determines if you are task dominant or share dominant.

Team members who are task dominant (Boomers and Gen Xers) are the wired generation and are anchored in a "manage me" feedback culture. Team members who are share dominant (Millennials and Gen Zers) are the wireless generation and are anchored in a "develop me" feedback culture.

Task-Dominant "Manage Me" Feedback

People who are task dominant traditionally experienced feedback that was given monthly or annually, either in person or on the phone. The phones in use until at least 2007 were connected by telephone lines to outlets in walls. The phones, and the people who used them, were tethered to desks. Employees working one-on-one with their managers eventually became accustomed to feedback as a tool for accountability. For example, they would participate in a 360 once a year and then use tools, including PowerPoint and Word, to demonstrate how they incorporated that feedback into the project or their career. Managers managed this group, and, in turn, members of the group managed their tasks independently; that is why this approach is called "manage me" feedback.

Share-Dominant "Develop Me" Feedback

Team members who are share dominant are accustomed to online access, meaning the Internet is seen as a group activity used to engage and communicate with thousands of people. Feedback is not a tool for accountability. Rather, it determines popularity. Feedback is a tool that allows Millennials and Gen Zers to be approachable and share online. This feedback experience is called the "develop me" approach.

People in the share-dominant generations generally check their phones and receive feedback every six minutes.[7] Since they are achievers, when they do not receive feedback from their teams or bosses, they will wonder what is going on. If the response is delayed for a longer time, they will begin to disengage. By the time the annual review comes around, it is too late. As a manager, to solve this problem, try the following, known as the instant conversation approach.

Work on providing daily feedback to your team. For group learning with a primarily Millennial team, these instant conversations work best on collaborative technology, such as Microsoft Teams or Slack. They work because they provide the group with data to make decisions, and they teach and lead by example. Here are two examples from my research:

1. Positive feedback given by a manager to a team member regarding a client meeting that went well: "Excellent work on presenting to Bob in the meeting today. Your approach was thorough and logical."

2. A corrective approach given by a manager to a team member after a meeting hadn't achieved its goals: "I noticed today that our client had multiple questions about the rollout, and we have a follow-up meeting next week. What are your ideas to prepare for that meeting, and how can we anticipate Sheehan's questions in the next meeting?" This feedback presents the problem and respectfully asks the team member for proposed solutions.

Fixing a Virtual Team's Damaged Culture

Now that you understand the instant conversation approach, you have the tools you need to change the negativity associated with staff reviews. If you have ever been through a 360 annual review, you know it is an agonizing time-suck for everyone involved. If you happen to work in a competitive culture, it also has the power to destroy your upward momentum. Every generation in today's workforce is experiencing digital feedback at unprecedented levels, yet critical feedback on their performance that affects their movement and chance at promotion only comes once a year. One high-achieving Millennial who attended my workshop on this topic summed it up nicely when he said to the group, "My company is big on 360s. I am not. It doesn't make sense. It's like my company saying they want me to be healthy, so they give me the opportunity to exercise once a year."

It's time to change. Instant feedback is upon us. Peter Cappelli and Anna Tavis, who wrote the *HBR* article "The Performance Management Revolution," mentioned in the previous chapter, found that by "providing people instant feedback, tying it to individuals' own goals, and handing out small weekly bonuses to employees they saw doing good things,"[8] change and retention were positively affected. But how do you do this when you are time starved, you have a system in place, and you don't want to buy any of the excellent new daily programs? Try the Donohue method in order to create more systematized conversation.

The Donohue method is an emerging management practice designed to defeat the negativity associated with feedback. It's deployed as a *team* feedback policy, versus an *individual* feedback policy, and an approach to weekly check-ins. This systematized conversation approach has proved successful as a collaborative performance appraisal format. Systematized conversation is employee "owned" and provides management with data, enabling decision making, based in real-time systematized conversation, to become a weekly check-in feedback tool that moves tasks and deliverables forward.

As a performance appraisal tool, it is built on the needs of the two dominant DEQs in the workplace today:

- **For the share dominant,** this systematized conversation meets the need for collaborative feedback that was constantly supplied by teachers, parents, and technology, which isn't being met with traditional once-a-year tools.

- **For the task dominant,** this systematized conversation meets the need to save time, understand who has done what, and create a record of those actions.

THERE IS NO NEED TO FEAR THE WORST

As humans, we all live for feedback. Unfortunately, digital is a very ineffective way to give it, and when the message given is not what the receiver anticipates, he or she fears the worst. We all want those nondigital social cues that don't exist in most digital communication, particularly when different generations are involved. As a sender, remember that people are fearing the worst, and probably reading the worst, out of your digital communications. Be aware of your digital body language, the anchoring benchmarks for the different generations, stress triggers to avoid, and sentence patterns to provide the desired response to the right generation. Remember that most feedback is perceived as something negative.

Thomas J. Watson, Sr., the founder of IBM, was a brilliant man who understood the value of culture, but in some ways, he was like Mike Duke, Walmart's former CEO, who didn't value the Internet's potential. According to Ernie Von Simson, Watson was slow to adapt to punch card technology because he was worried it would kill IBM's business. Thomas J. Watson, Jr., however, had other ideas that allowed his team to adapt to the second generation of computers, which were showpieces in data centers all over the world. Watson, Jr., knew how to build and motivate a team because he was able to master the art of the collaboration game, allowing IBM to dominate the brave new world of data.

Understanding your team's cultural stress points and working out the bugs in your culture will enable you to have some fun at work through collaboration, using digital to draw out each generation's best skills. To do this, use feedback with your team that incorporates DEQ and creates transparency. It will never fail to ignite collaboration as long as you avoid the barriers that waste time in meetings, as discussed in the next chapter.

CHAPTER FIVE

STEP 5:
HAVE BETTER MEETINGS

THE OSBORN TOUCH

In 1919 Alex F. Osborn became one of the three founders of an advertising agency called BBDO. All went well until one of his partners decided to leave the company in 1939 and strike out on his own. This was bad news for the business. Mr. Osborn needed to drive revenue, which he knew wasn't going to be easy because the US economy was still feeling the effects of the Great Depression. Osborn began to wonder how he could get more creativity from his employees—he needed them to think up new ideas so the company could win new business. He wanted his agency to be the most creative team in town.

Eventually, he came up with the concept of a "thinking-up meeting," which today we call a brainstorming meeting. It worked spectacularly well. By 1951 BBDO had become the second advertising agency in the United States of America to pass $100 million in billings. And according to Hanisha Besant, writing in the *Journal of Transformative Innovation* in 1953, Osborn introduced the process of brainstorming, along with illustrations of BBDO's success stories, in *Applied Imagination*.[1] What made Osborn's system so successful was that he systematized the meeting with strict rules that had to be followed and limited the number of people in the thinking-up sessions to between 5 and 12. Today, meetings unquestionably need the *Osborn touch*. We need a system with rules that keeps everyone on track and on time.

MEETINGS AND THE FATIGUE HUMP

The World Health Organization lists the first symptom of burnout as "feelings of energy depletion or exhaustion."[2] Nowhere are these symptoms more evident in the workplace than in our perception of, and participation in, meetings. Rather than streamlining the experience of meetings, digital has exacerbated the problem of meetings. Meetings already feel too long and don't always add value to our work. Also, depending on our generation, the technology options for "meeting" can be annoying. When combined with the stress of too many emails, assumption, and lack of trust, the multitude of meetings we attend is exhausting us and causing meeting fatigue. To reduce this exhaustion, this chapter will provide tips to systematize your meetings by using technology, common sense, and the science of generational anchoring benchmarks.

DEFINING THE PROBLEMS WITH MEETINGS

Research has demonstrated we need shorter and more humanized meetings.[3] We like meetings and connecting with others, but we don't like how meetings are conducted. In order to understand what we dislike about meetings, I worked with ConStat and Microsoft, which conducted a survey of 800 executives, asking them how they experience and feel about meetings. Here's what I learned:

- The average meeting lasts 60 minutes, and the *minimum* number attended by any generation is 10 per week.

- Organizations often engage in pre-meetings to discuss an upcoming meeting and then schedule post-meetings to ensure next steps are clear and deliverables are assigned.

- In an average week, our survey respondents spend 36 hours on a laptop and attend 10 meetings, and those same respondents organize just over half of the meetings they attend.

- Of these meetings, 45 percent are in person, 32 percent are virtual, and 22 percent are a mix of in-person meetings and virtual meetings.

- Almost half of all participants regularly call into a meeting or work remotely.

- Participants send emails to other team members to hold a pre-meeting about an upcoming meeting. This occurs because it is not clear to participants why a meeting is being held. Much time is wasted in this process.

- In general, only 17 percent of us are happy with the way meetings are held and their outcomes.

- Team members aren't using meetings' minutes to move a project forward and are not assigning to-dos during meetings.

- The majority of meeting participants have observed that too many people are multitasking in meetings and failing to move an item forward.

By sorting through all of this information, I found three basic reasons why meetings are exhausting us: one, technology nuisances; two, length and frequency of meetings; and three, the lack of value of meetings. Let's break each down a little further.

Technology Nuisances

The advent of the smartphone in 2007 didn't just change how we communicate but also changed the physicality of meetings. According to the Wisconsin Hospital Association, in the past we held meetings "to discuss something face to face. It could be a new idea, a new opportunity, a problem, to brainstorm something, reach a decision about something or any number of things. But it all comes down to discussion and face-to-face interaction."[4]

Today, we have lost that in-person, face-to-face interaction because we use digital tools to conduct meetings. A participant in the research I conducted for Microsoft explained this change at her company: "Everybody used to meet face-to-face, and we spent bags and bags of money on travel, and we just don't do that anymore." Companies can't afford that many face-to-face meetings, but they want to increase productivity quarter over quarter; therefore, they are increasing the number of meetings held and the technology to "track" the value of these meetings. Boomers and Gen X team members, who make up over 50 percent of the workforce, are finding this a nuisance, as explained to me by this Gen Xer:

> There are a number of different client management tools. That is, if you want to call them tools. I call them *nuisances* at times. But there is really a kind of micromanagement that you have to deal with. The company wants to see activity and productivity in one manner or another, besides just the revenue that you bring in . . . I call it the matrix measurement, where, in lieu

of revenue (we don't have that problem), they want to see a lot of activity, meetings, calls, conferences. But even with high revenue, they still want to see that activity. Squeeze as much productivity as you can out of each employee [is] what I've noticed compared to [when] I got in our business. I'm probably quite a bit older, but going back in the early to the mid-'90s, our job was to pick up a phone and start calling people.[5]

Length and Frequency

Over the past few years, research on meetings and meeting trends, like video conferencing huddles, has shown that huddle rooms have become a hot-button topic for agile workforces. Bain & Company wrote a piece in *Harvard Business Review* in 2014 that ignited interest in the topic of time wasted in meetings, and since then, Deloitte and Environics have also weighed in. Bain found that, on average, senior executives devote more than two days every week to meetings involving three or more coworkers, and 15 percent of an organization's collective time is spent in meetings—a percentage that has increased every year since 2008.[6] The length of meetings depends on the type of meeting, as indicated in Table 5.1.

TABLE 5.1: **Meeting Type and Length**

Meeting Type	Average Length of Meeting (as Reported by Participants)
Collaboration meeting	60+ minutes
Status meeting	Less than 30 minutes
Customer-focused meeting	30–60 minutes
Learning meeting	30–60 minutes
Formal meeting	60+ minutes

Lack of Value

Compounding the problem of both technology and the frequency of meetings is the fact that 37 percent of us believe that overly frequent meetings lack value.[7] This quote from a participant in my research seems to sum up the frustration many others also feel:

> I go to a lot of unproductive meetings. The people internally that I invite are not prepared. They don't do any research even though I gave them the materials that we were going to talk about and why. They show up and have no idea. That's frustrating. There's a lot of repetition. One person says something and then somebody else repeats it in a different way to show that they also have value at this company.

The data clearly show that meetings do not always lead to productivity. And one of the biggest reasons meetings aren't effective is that everyone has a different understanding of each meeting's purpose. Because of this, we experience roadblocks in communication. Breaking down these roadblocks can be done by systematizing and humanizing meetings. The former is accomplished by using generational preferences, complemented with structure.

GENERATIONS AND MEETING PREFERENCES

Meetings are defined differently by each generation. What one generation understands as a status meeting, another generation views as an opportunity to collaborate; as a result, frustration naturally occurs. Meetings are viewed by each generation through the lenses of education and leadership trends. This colors how each generation views meeting technology and the need for and length of a meeting, as well as what constitutes a valuable meeting. Much as we've discussed so far, you can probably guess the communication style of someone by how they act in a meeting. Going back to our task-default and share-default communication styles, we can categorize the differences by generation members' perceptions of meetings.

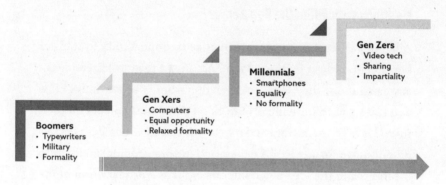

FIGURE 5.1: The Evolution of Generational Meeting Preferences

Meetings with Ben the Boomer

Ben, like most Boomers, views meetings as an opportunity for all team members to become informed. Boomers particularly like status meetings because they enjoy formality in a meeting. To them, a wasted meeting results from participants talking too much, not sticking to the agenda, and ignoring the person who has the floor. Boomers prefer more formal meetings, as they were educated in a very strict high school regimen. There were rules and, in some cases, corporal punishment. The first meetings they attended had formal rules. In high school, the norm for all Boomers was that there were consequences for not studying, including failure, shame, and suspension. Postsecondary education was a privilege, and primarily men attended.

Punishment for not following the rules was harsh. Boomers, therefore, get geared up for meetings and expect others to be as well. They expect there to be consequences if someone is not prepared for, or fails to attend, a meeting. They also expect that those with title or seniority will naturally lead the meeting.

Meetings with Adam the Gen Xer

Adam, as a Gen Xer, views meetings as an opportunity to transfer knowledge and get on track. Gen Xers attend the most meetings of any generation. They see them as an opportunity to get things done as a team and to individually check off some of the items on their to-do lists. To them, a wasted meeting is one in which deliverables do not move forward. This generation introduced informality into meetings and the idea of a conference call as a primary tool in the workplace. They prefer to participate in these meetings with their hard copy notebooks and pens handy so they can take notes. Gen Xers didn't have the same harsh regimen at school that Boomers had. There was no corporal punishment, and truancy became the parents' responsibility. Men and women were equally welcome at colleges and universities.

Competition became the way to challenge students, and therefore, winning became the key to success. Individualism was important, but in order to win, you had to demonstrate that you were a team player. Power was recognized as being in the hands of the experts, who were not averse to shaming underperformers in an effort to motivate them.

Gen Xers view meetings as a task that needs to be completed in order to win, because with winning comes control. Preparation is important, but it is also important to speak up in a meeting to show that you are a team player and a winner. Gen Xers enjoy leading meetings because it means they have control of the meetings.

Meetings with Trish the Millennial and Tyler the Gen Zer

Both Trish and Tyler, our Millennial and Gen Zer, were educated differently than previous generations. They were educated in teams because of the limited financial resources available to school boards. Teachers were less often acknowledged formally as "Sir" or "Ms." and, instead, called by their first names. As teachers dressed less formally, formality ceased in public education. Positive feedback, and not shaming, was encouraged.

Problem solving as a team and as a participant within the team became the norm. Computer and online sharing also emerged, and by the time Millennials were in postsecondary programs, accessing lecture materials and working as a team online was the norm.

This more informal and friendlier approach to learning was transferred to the workplace; meeting times became more flexible as long as the necessary work was completed prior to the deadline. Materials were reviewed in a meeting, and then the team discussed them, much as they had in a classroom. Millennials' and Gen Zers' meetings are less rigid and formal than Boomers' and Gen Xers'.

Just as school became less formal, work became less driven by the human touch and more about the digital drive.

With these dramatic differences among team members, meetings were going to suffer as communication patterns were no longer homogeneous. In order to standardize patterns, it's important to create a classification system for your meetings, as ConStat discovered in our research together. Let's dive into each meeting type now.

THE FIVE TYPES OF MEETINGS

In my research with ConStat and subsequent client-based focus groups, we found that all generations agreed that there were five different types of meetings. They are:

1. Collaboration

2. Status

3. Customer focused

4. Learning

5. Formal

I would like to add a disclaimer here that Gen Zers aren't mentioned in the meeting preference types below because, statistically, they aren't a large enough group to be measured just yet. The meetings are defined by their characteristics and some real "ah-ha" moments discovered during the research.

TABLE 5.2: **Meetings Defined**

Meeting Categories	Definition	Generational Insight
Collaboration	Brainstorming, ideation, and problem solving	Millennials attend remotely and have higher interaction
Status	Review projects, plan new schedules, and report on deliverables	Boomers love status meetings and scored highest in interaction levels in this type of meeting

Meeting Categories	Definition	Generational Insight
Customer Focused	External facing meeting for sales, support, and service	Gen Xers enjoy time with customers; their problem is getting time with customers, both external and internal
Learning	Characterized by training, learning and development, and sharing of new information; often a mentoring meeting	Millennials and Boomers enjoy classes but are frustrated by no follow-up after training
Formal	Typical "all hands-on deck," town hall–type meeting	Disliked by all generations

Collaboration Meetings

- Designed for brainstorming, ideation, and problem solving.

- One of the most frequently attended type of meetings: 90 percent of all employees attend collaboration meetings.

- About one-fifth (22 percent) of all meetings in a company are collaboration meetings.

- Tend to be longer than other types of meetings (60 minutes or longer in duration) and have a higher level of interaction.

- Documents are revised during these meetings.

- Require the most technical support of all meetings, such as access to files, email, calendars, whiteboards, and support software.

- Less likely to start on time.

- Attendees often multitask during these meetings.

- Current satisfaction with the collaboration meeting is quite high (75 percent).

Status Meetings

- Ongoing meetings to review projects, plan new schedules, and report on deliverables.

- Almost all employees attend meetings of this type (91 percent).

- The most frequent meetings attended within an organization (27 percent of all meetings).

- Tend to be the shortest meetings (30 percent are less than 30 minutes).

- Less likely to have an agenda.

- Of all the meeting types, more than any other, people surveyed felt that "there are too many of these types of meetings."

- Have the lowest use of video teleconferencing (VTC) systems, video presentations, and digital note-taking tools.

- Current satisfaction is "in the middle" (71 percent).

- Tend to feature little sidebar communication among participants.

Customer-Focused Meetings

- Both internal and external: internal discussion meetings are about planning to meet with customers, and external-facing meetings, including webinars, are for sales, support, and service.

- Usually attended only by customer-facing employees. Less than three-fourths of employees attend these meetings.

- Relatively infrequent meetings across the entire organization (18 percent).

- Usually include the lowest number of people.

- Tend to be a longer type of meeting (85 percent are over 30 minutes in duration, up to 90 minutes).

- Most likely type to have an agenda.

- Most likely to have pre-meeting email communications and materials sent out in advance.

- Most likely to have people from outside the organization in attendance.

- Have the highest satisfaction among all meetings (77 percent).

Learning Meetings

- Characterized by training, learning and development, and sharing of new information.

- Most employees attend this type of meeting (87 percent), but fewer than the collaboration or status meetings.

- Less than one-fifth (19 percent) of all meetings in a company are of this type.

- Tend to be short (80 percent are less than 60 minutes in duration but more than 30 minutes).

- Tend to have more attendees than all meetings except formal ones.

- Less likely to have emails or materials sent out in advance.

- Less likely to have follow-ups.

- A mid-level of tech support is needed.

- Satisfaction and productivity with this type of meeting are rated relatively low.

- Participants often feel that others don't come properly prepared.

Formal Meetings

- The typical "all hands-on deck," town hall–type meeting, usually involving a major corporate presentation or announcement.

- Surprisingly, relatively low level of participation (only 81 percent attend these meetings) and lowest level of interaction.

- Least frequent type of meeting (12 percent) and by far the largest in terms of attendees.

- Most participants attend in person (65 percent).

- Longest type of meeting (41 percent run over 60 minutes).

- Have the highest use of VTC systems.

- Often take place in an auditorium or a large room and utilize video presentations.

- Have the lowest level of tech support for attendees.

- Have the lowest level of satisfaction (65 percent) and productivity (62 percent).

Now let's take a look at each generation's preferred meeting type and understand their different stress triggers within meetings.

Collaboration Meetings: The Millennials' Favorite (Followed Closely by Gen Xers' and Likely Gen Zers')

These meetings are designed for brainstorming, ideation, and problem solving, and Millennials (share default) are the most satisfied of all generations with these types of meetings. The technology they prefer for participating in these meetings is their phones. When a collaboration meeting causes stress for a Millennial, it's because the meeting is too long. Millennials will lose interest and perceive lost value in a meeting when their bosses are multitasking; however, as a group they do like to revise documents "live" during meetings and exchange emojis and instant messages with other attendees.

Status Meetings: Boomers' Favorite (Followed Closely by Gen Xers')

These are ongoing meetings to review projects, plan new schedules, and report on deliverables. Boomers (who are task default) are the most satisfied of all generations with these types of meetings. Boomers prefer to meet face-to-face for status meetings; however, when this isn't possible, they will dial into a meeting. When a status meeting causes stress for a Boomer it's because others came to the meeting unprepared. Boomers will lose interest and perceive lost value when attendees show up late, or don't show up at all, to a status meeting.

Customer-Focused Meetings: Gen Xers' Favorite (Followed Closely by Boomers')

These types of meetings may be internal meetings with your internal customer-servicing team or external-facing meetings for sales, support, and service staff. Both the internal customer-focused meeting, sometimes known as the pre-meeting, and the actual meeting with the customer are designed for selling to clients, solving a client problem, or maintaining and growing a client's account. Gen Xers (task default) are the most satisfied of all generations with these types of meetings. They enjoy problem solving. The technology they use is either a web solution on a laptop or a mobile app. They prefer to access information for customer meetings through electronic or handwritten notes. Gen Xers will lose interest and perceive lost value when the meetings last too long or when they take too long to plan with others through technology in the first place.

Learning Meetings: Millennials' and Boomers' Second Favorite

These types of meetings are characterized by training, learning and development, and sharing of new information. Millennials (share default) and Boomers (task default) are the two generations that are most satisfied with learning meetings. Both generations prefer meeting face-to-face. They experience stress when people don't come prepared to training and when the training goes on too long. They perceive lost value in these meetings when there is no follow-up to the training. Gen Xers struggle with finding the time to attend these meetings.

Formal Meetings: No One's Favorite

These are the typical "all hands-on deck," town hall–type meetings. They usually involve a major corporate presentation or announcement. None of the generations surveyed had a positive opinion on formal meetings. The primary goal of these meetings is to ignite the creation of better or more effective processes, services, and technologies.

We found that participants believe meetings are a good use of time when they meet their generational expectations for structure and participation, but we can't always create meetings to meet everyone's needs—that would really be exhausting. So how do we deal with this?

HOW TO RUN A SUCCESSFUL MEETING

To run a productive meeting, you have to understand how to prepare for the meeting, run the meeting, and determine post-meeting actions. Let's look deeper into each of these steps.

Step One: Create a Pre-Meeting Assessment

Before you even suggest a meeting, determine if it's necessary. Really ask yourself, or your team, to determine the purpose of the meeting. Is it to make a decision? Is it to inform people? Next, ask yourself if no one attended this meeting or if you didn't have it, would it matter? Last, ask yourself what success will look like for this meeting.

Based on these answers, you'll be able to determine if the meeting is important and which of the five meeting types you will be conducting. The primary goal of each meeting type is one of the following:

- **Information sharing:** To communicate necessary or new information about a specific project.

- **Team building:** To engage team members and demonstrate that they are, or will become, essential members of the team; a brainstorming session to build culture.

- **Status:** To deliver a brief update on a current project or advise changes to deadlines.

- **Decision making:** To walk away with a clear and final direction to move forward; a customer meeting.

- **Problem solving:** To resolve a specific or general problem that is crucial to the project, team, or company.

Once you have determined what type of meeting you are hosting, create a calendar invite with an appropriate subject line, including the type of meeting (for example, "Corporate Goal-Setting, Decision-Making Meeting").

Next, manage people's expectations by letting them know how much of their day you will need for the meeting. The length of a meeting should be determined by the goals, or intended outcomes, and their level of significance. The following list includes some suggested times for each type of meeting:

- Collaboration meetings: 15 minutes to a full day

- Status meetings: 15 to 30 minutes

- Customer-focused meetings: 30 to 60 minutes

- Learning meetings: 90 minutes to a full day

- Formal meetings: 10 to 60 minutes

Once you have determined how long your meeting should be, choose that time frame in your meeting invite. Last, include the necessary materials and details that participants should know, bring, or review. These could include any or all of the following:

- Meeting location (for an off-site meeting, provide a map and directions to parking lots, along with public transit options)

- Technology being used and a quick "how-to" sheet

- Agenda with start and finish times

- List of who will be speaking or presenting and time frames for each

- Date and time by when participants must review all information

- Due dates for specific people and content

These steps will result in a perfect pre-meeting calendar invite for all generations. To be extra considerate, I also suggest sending the information in PDF format so participants who are flying to the meeting and preparing on the plane can prepare without having to be connected to Wi-Fi.

Step Two: Create a Structure for the Meeting

By being aware of generational meeting preferences, you can avoid stress triggers for participants by structuring your meetings effectively, sharing the necessary information, and running every meeting in the exact same manner.

Based on the research conducted with ConStat and Microsoft, the most successful meeting structure is described as follows:

1. **Appoint a timekeeper:** Before the meeting, determine who will keep track of time to manage the agenda. Also, tell participants that this person will not just track but also indicate their remaining time (for example, by raising his or her hand when a speaker has five minutes left or holding up two fingers at the two-minutes-left mark).

2. **Introduce team members:** Introduce team members and include photos for those who are not attending in person. Ensure that participants have a visual of who is speaking.

3. **Manage discussions:** In order for everyone to speak and to know who is speaking, encourage participants to identify themselves before they make a comment.

4. **Record the meeting:** This step is crucial because written minutes or a recording of each meeting allows attendees to reference important discussions and potential action items at a later date. Just remember to tell everyone the meeting will be recorded.

At the end of the meeting, create a calendar invite that reminds participants of any determined deadlines or completion dates. Our beta group found it helpful to encourage team members to use their smartphones or laptops to accept meeting tasks while still *in* the meeting.

Step Three: Determine Post-Meeting Actions

When the meeting is over, the work begins. The post-meeting review is an essential component of the meeting. This short email of 200 words can recap decisions made, call out innovative ideas, remind participants of deadlines, or invite more great ideas. Doing this meets the needs of all the generations, as it reminds them of why they attended the meeting and the value of collaboration.

➤

To make all of this even easier for you, Figure 5.2 provides a checklist you can use to run a great meeting.

Conducting a Meeting Checklist	
Pre-Meeting	
✓	Identify purpose of meeting: information sharing, team building, status, decision making, or problem solving
	Prepare an agenda
	Select format (face-to-face vs. virtual)
	Choose technology based on generational profile of attendees (e.g., Zoom or Teams)
	Ensure all members are familiar with the technology, and if not, send a quick "how-to" sheet
	Set the level of participation required
	Create a calendar invite and send, along with pre-meeting materials
During the Meeting	
✓	Record the meeting or archive it (e.g., use built-in technology, such as Zoom's record option)
	Introduce team members and include photos for those attending virtually
	Appoint a timekeeper to manage the agenda
	Run the meeting and manage discussions
	Determine next steps
	Create a calendar invite that reminds participants of the completion dates of action items
Post-Meeting	
	Send out review and next steps via email

FIGURE 5.2: Meeting Checklist

AVOID TYPICAL MEETING ROADBLOCKS

As the old saying goes, forewarned is forearmed. The following are three barriers that occur in meetings and three solutions to those barriers to create more productive meetings.

Barrier #1: Multitasking

Solution #1: Embrace Osborn's Rules

Boomer-aged employees (and some older Gen X workers) complain that many attendees multitask during meetings because they see them using smartphones, laptops, or tablets—all of which can be used for anything from note-taking to surfing the web to checking information that is being discussed. While Boomers are for the most part against multitasking, younger generations are not.

So in order to make sure everyone is on the same page and gets the most out of meetings, I suggest you send the following note and rules to participants before any meeting:

Hi everyone. In order to accomplish everything we need to do today, please adhere to the following meeting rules. When we are all digitally present, we are all also "digitally heard," so please be aware of the noise you may be creating in the background during the meeting. If you have any suggestions for the rules, please let me know:

1. **Do:** Click the comment or chat button right away if you have something to say. Don't wait. I am happy to stop my presentation for discussion.

2. **Don't** use your computer to do other tasks. Others can hear you do this. It sends the message that you don't really care about being present in this meeting and you are not listening to what other team members have to say.

3. **Do:** Commit to the digital meeting. It is valuable.

4. **Don't** worry if we have to change our meeting time. Life happens, but I really look forward to rescheduling. If this doesn't work for you, let me know. Happy to jump on a quick call, or text me at [insert cell phone number].

5. **Do:** Put yourself on mute when you are not speaking. Even if you aren't typing, there can be static coming from your line that is disturbing to others.

As a reminder, our meetings are to end on time and/or early.

Thank you,

M

Unless all meeting attendees put their phones aside, with the notifications function turned off, you won't be able to stop sidebarring. Alert participants to the fact that their desire to have private conversations will not override the rules of the meeting.

Barrier #2: Meetings That Are Too Long

Solution: Embrace Video

Video allows the meeting leader to minimize the negative effects of disengagement. Video meetings can be timed and cut off abruptly when time is up. For example, during the COVID-19 crisis, my team and I would use Zoom, and I would put a timer on my screen. Some team members wanted to chat, but everyone was aware of the time we had left on the call, during which we needed to get our client deliverables completed. Although in the beginning some team members, particularly my teammate Don, a Boomer, found this timer to be stressful, the team enjoyed it when the meetings ended early.

Video meetings, using technology such as Webex, have options that allow us to very clearly demonstrate the time we have together while also allowing all participants to be seen. The only technology that is needed aside from the video conferencing or calling app is the camera on your computer. A funny aside about cameras is that we found many Gen Xers and Boomers had put pieces of tape over their laptops' cameras. As much as they did not want to be seen by others, others did want to see them and engage with them—it helps us all to be more human. When we see others, and are seen by them, during a meeting, our manners seem to return, and we start participating rather than focusing on something else.

Barrier #3: People Are Not Prepared

Solution: Embrace Achiever Aids

In my research, I learned that people in certain industries, such as banking, are trained to be prepared for meetings. However, for those who aren't, the solution is to use achiever aids, or reminders, to prepare for meetings. On average, we attend 10 meetings a week, so anything that can be done to help people participate in a meeting more fully will generate higher productivity and assure that more people are prepared.

I found that less than one-third of attendees fail to read pre-meeting materials. Creating short videos outlining the agenda and expected outcomes of an upcoming meeting will help productivity too. Another solution is to give participants time at the start of the meeting to read the material. Since we are all typically running from one meeting to the next and answering emails in between, this time allows participants the chance to breathe and read.

THE SECRET TO A GOOD LIFE AT WORK

No matter where we work or our position, we are social beings who need to meet, whether formally or informally. Meetings are our connection to others in the organization. That's why we like meetings, because they are part of the human ethos. The secret to life at work is understanding how to organize, engage, run, and operate a successful meeting so that when we do meet, we don't feel like we've wasted our time or that we haven't been heard.

A great meeting is a highpoint in breaking the barriers for communication, because if we can get meetings right, we are ready to break down generational collaboration barriers, the topic of the next chapter.

CHAPTER SIX

STEP 6:
AMPLIFY GENERATIONAL
COLLABORATION
WITH MENTORING

AMPLIFICATION

As we learned in the Introduction, people spend four hours a day in meetings, working with others. This is commonly known as collaboration, and when done well, it results in better ideas, increased productivity, and a higher quality of work. But how do we get generations to collaborate effectively when it feels like we're all dealing with collaboration overload?

Research from the Pew Research Center,[1] Deloitte,[2] and others, such as *Training Industry* magazine,[3] suggest that to amplify generational collaboration we should adapt a formal or informal mentoring program. Mentoring aligns with the cultural expectations of Millennials and Gen Zers. And when we use mentoring as a tool for collaboration, it cultivates intergenerational creative partnerships and intellectual stimulation.

Identify Generational Collaboration Motivators

The first step to collaboration is to engage people in the process— and the way to do this is to understand what motivates them. And as we've learned throughout this book, each generation has its own set of motivations, so in order to collaborate effectively, you need to understand their collaboration motivators.

Collaboration motivators are the triggers that stimulate collaboration and break down barriers. Each generation's anchoring benchmarks underpin its collaboration motivators, outlined in Table 6.1, which we'll come to understand in the following sections.

TABLE 6.1: **Generational Anchoring Benchmarks: Collaboration Motivators**

	Collaboration Motivators	Triggers
Boomers	The American Dream	Use examples of how people like them achieved success and offer executive perks and public praise for a job well done
Gen Xers	Self-preservation	Give them the guidelines for collaboration and then explain what "winning" looks like and how it will benefit them and the team.
Millennials	Learning	This is a very civically aware generation, motivated to collaborate to help others—it is how they learned; align with the triggers of civic duty and how it will help the team and community
Gen Zers	Truth and equality for all	Nondiscriminatory practices, clear standards, and norms that guide collaboration

Boomers' Collaboration Motivator: The American Dream

As with all Boomers, Ben's collaboration motivator is the American Dream, the "promise" made to them as children that they, just like anyone in America, could achieve their goals and make their dreams come true. This promise was made by parents, politicians, and even advertisers. As children, Boomers were told by advertisers that if you bought certain products, they would help you achieve success. Incidentally, advertisers still use this methodology today, which they call demographic segmentation—it's how they get people to buy products and services. The American Dream is Boomers' collaboration authority; it is the assumption that underpins their world. When you want to reduce collaboration barriers with Boomers, align with the trigger of the American Dream. Use examples of how people like them achieved success and offer executive perks and public praise for a job well done—signs of achieving the American Dream.

Gen Xers' Collaboration Motivator: Self-Preservation

Like all other Gen Xers, Adam's collaboration motivator is based in the reality of money. As Gen Xers were growing up and entering the workforce, they saw the political fallout from Watergate, the effects of the energy crisis, and their parents become victims of corporate mergers and downsizing. Their collaboration trigger is self-preservation: protect yourself, your family, and your team. Politicians began to realize this and promote it. Parents encouraged independence at an early age. After my brothers and I left for college, my parents moved to a very small home. We were told we were welcome to visit, but there was nowhere for us to sleep for any length of time. My parents offered couches and one particularly uncomfortable bed. As funny as this might sound today, it didn't seem strange to my brothers and me or to our friends. Our parents wanted to get on with their lives, and their message to us was, "You will survive. You don't need to depend on us."

When you want to reduce collaboration barriers with Gen Xers, align with the trigger of self-preservation and team preservation. Give them the guidelines for collaboration and then explain what "winning" looks like and how it will benefit them and the team. Remember, this is the generation whose motto is "work hard, play hard."

Millennials' Collaboration Motivator: Learning

Trish's collaboration motivator, like most Millennials', is learning. Millennials were members of the first generation to experience volunteering as part of their learning journey. They were also the first to have mentors, tutors, and coaches for every aspect of learning. They constantly strive to learn more, and they often work in groups to achieve this. As the first generation to volunteer, they also have a profound sense of community. This sense of community also drives an awareness, or heightened awareness, of family and self. This gives them the strength and power to strive for a work-life balance. Unlike their older Gen X siblings, this generation understands the importance of "time away," and they are excited to explore all life has to offer them.

Their collaboration trigger has created a generation that has very high collaboration standards, and they have a far more global view of the world than previous generations. Their parents and teachers reinforced this, and so did Facebook. With the introduction of social media, Millennials could "see and hear" what was happening outside of their immediate world. Couple this with the fact that this generation was given school credit for volunteering, and you have a civically aware, motivated generation that often collaborates together to help others. When you want to reduce the collaboration barriers with Millennials, align with the triggers of self-love and civic duty.

Gen Zers' Collaboration Motivator: Truth and Equality for All

Tyler, like all other Gen Zers, was parented by people whose lives were turned upside down by the 2007–2008 great recession. This generation's collaboration motivator is truth, a fundamental belief in right and wrong, as it benefits everyone. Only a few members of the Gen Z cohort were born pre-9/11, and as a result, most have never known a world without terrorism. This has shaped their collaboration preferences around the principles of right and wrong and equality for all. More than any other generation, Gen Zers follow rules very well. As a consequence, when others break the rules and aren't punished, Gen Zers have no problem withdrawing from the collaboration process or jumping into action and reporting them. When people break the rules, no matter their position in the company, research tells us that Gen Zers will immediately disengage.

They believe in equity for all and are far more likely than any other generation to fight for a society that is nondiscriminatory. To break down collaboration barriers with this generation, demonstrate equal opportunities for success. For example, ensure that your diverse leaders have a voice. Replace high-potential programs with mentoring and coaching programs. But if you *must* have a high-potential program, ensure that everyone can apply to the program and then explain the results.

Amplify Collaboration by Increasing Productivity

Each generation's collaboration motivators are important in getting teams to clearly communicate. But if you really want to increase productivity—defined as creative partnerships, critical thinking, and problem solving—mentoring is key. Research from scientists, academics, and professional services firms has found that collaboration is more productive when a mentoring relationship is present. Writing in the academic journal *Implementation Science*, the authors found that between scientists, mentoring relationships increased productivity—defined as grant submissions, publications, and future collaboration—by 7 percent.[4]

Mentoring increases productivity because it reduces **organizational drag**. Michael Mankins, writing in *Harvard Business Review*, defined organizational drag as the structures and processes that prevent people from getting things done. He found that "the average company loses more than 20% of its productive capacity—more than a day each week—to what we call organizational drag."[5] Mentoring increases productivity by 10 percent,[6] reducing organizational drag by teaching team members how to work through the bureaucratic process, which increases job satisfaction, motivation, and, subsequently, output (productivity).

But how do you build mentoring into collaboration, particularly digital collaboration, to ensure it is productive? You build in mentoring motivators.

Mentoring is a generational productivity tool that breaks down collaboration barriers by aligning collaborations through conversation. Let's explore what mentoring is and how the different generations respond to it.

For Millennials and Gen Zers, mentoring is a collaboration vehicle and a natural extension of their share-dominant or "develop me" DEQ (discussed in the Introduction and Chapter 4). For Gen Xers and Boomers, mentoring satisfies their task-dominant or "manage me" DEQ (also discussed in the Introduction and Chapter 4) because it is a proven tool to increase productivity. The key to ramping up collaboration through mentoring is to understand how each generation is inspired by mentoring or to mentor.

MENTORING: OPTIMUM COLLABORATION ACROSS GENERATIONS

According to Peter Martel, a senior talent development consultant at Harvard Business School, "in businesses with highly engaged teams, profitability increased by 21 percent, sales productivity by 20 percent, and output quality by 40 percent."[7] Mentoring increases engagement because both mentors and mentees learn about and from each other. Together, this relationship results in all-around success in an organization. And, as mentioned earlier, when mentoring is used as a tool for collaboration, it nurtures intergenerational partnerships and intellectual stimulation, as it did for the scientists when it increased their productivity by 7 percent.

Mentoring amplifies collaboration in both new and established teams because it enables both mentors and mentees to have their creative needs met, and it allows all parties to be heard. Mentoring is a vehicle for self-fulfillment. For example, mentoring:

- Acknowledges Boomers' knowledge and enables them to pass on that knowledge and build their legacy.

- Helps Gen Xers remember just how much they know and assures them that they are valued in their organization.

- Meets Millennials' need to develop and self-actualize at work.

- Gives Gen Zers an opportunity to learn about, and in, the culture of the workplace in which they thrive.

Mentoring Motivators

Think of mentoring as a fitness program for a more collaborative, productive, and healthier team. Like a good fitness program, a good mentoring program needs focus. This is done by providing structure through a variety of structured conversations, or exercises, to get the most out of the experience. Structure meets the generational needs of each group member on your team. For example:

- Boomers like structure because it keeps them on track.

- Gen Xers appreciate structure because they know what to expect and can just jump into it without too much preparation, which addresses their fear of missing out on work.

- Millennials and Gen Zers expect structure.

To build your structure, use the mentoring conversations at the end of this chapter to begin customizing your mentoring program and breaking down collaboration barriers. But before you get there, Table 6.2 will help you understand the mentoring motivators for each generation, their preferred mentoring styles, and their collaboration motivators.

In the table, you will notice I use two terms: **one-on-one mentoring** and **mentoring circles**. One-on-one mentoring is preferred by Boomers and Gen Xers and is what is known as traditional mentoring, where one person acts as a mentor and the other person as the mentee. Mentoring circles are a far more cost-effective method for mentoring and are the preference for Millennials and Gen Zers. Mentoring circles engage Millennials and Gen Zers in a group-learning format they are familiar with.

A client who had to merge two cultures together after a corporate takeover called on me to help break down barriers by using mentoring circles. Mentoring circles occur when one leader who acts as the mentor is paired with two to three mentees. Each month, the group spends one hour in a sharing-learning conversation, which has an agenda and goal. For this client, the circles worked very well. The

TABLE 6.2: **Preferred Generational Mentoring Styles and Collaboration Motivators**

Generation	Mentoring Personality	Mentoring Preference	Mentoring Motivator	Collaboration Motivator
Boomer	Honorable leaders	One-on-one, in person	It is my job to train others, seeing that staff are developed and have the right skills to benefit the company	The American Dream: I am helping others achieve their dreams and ambitions
Gen X	Command-and-control	One-on-one, on the phone or digitally	It is my job to help others understand the culture and ethics of our organization; this will benefit the company by creating a cohesive team	Self-preservation: I am sharing my understanding of the company and how to get "stuff" done, which will increase productivity and collaboration
Millennial	Democratic	Mentoring circles, in person or digitally	It is my job to learn and teach others new skills; mentoring others will help me advance my career and help others develop in their current position and advance too	Learning: mentoring will help me develop and better understand how to thrive in this organization or another
Gen Z	Equalitarian	Mentoring circles, in person or digitally	It is my job to learn new skills, socialize, share; mentoring circles bring three or more people together to learn from one another, shaping the desired outcomes of the experience	Truth and equality for all: mentoring together will create a stronger company and personal experience

first group to go through this process consisted primarily of older Millennials and Gen Xers; 61 percent of the group received a promotion within five months of beginning the program. The mentoring circles were so cost effective that the new company continued to use them for two years.[8]

Boomers' Mentoring Motivator

When you need to improve a team's productivity, give the task to a Boomer. I refer to Boomers as "natural builders" because they have experience with management. Using mentoring, Boomers can easily and quickly build or repair productivity in a team because they understand the value of soft skills for team collaboration. Boomer mentors like the legacy of training others not just in soft skills but in cultural fluency—it's a natural process for them. Boomers realize that developed staff, who have the skills to handle the job, will benefit the company.

Gen Xers' Mentoring Motivator

Gen Xers understand the value of a cohesive team, one that gels and "just gets it." As mentors, they focus on skills and methods needed for working across various departments, such as HR or IT. Gen Xers are the creators of an organization's cultural road map. As mentors, Gen Xers focus on sharing skills that help others grow and enable them to excel at their jobs. They teach their mentees to find out what is broken and fix it, on time and on budget.

Millennials' Mentoring Motivator

When you need to modernize or rebuild a team, call on a Millennial. The Millennial generation is the most adaptable one. Many Millennials have acted in the role of mentor to help team members learn technology and new "digital skills." As mentors, Millennials have no ego. Our epitome of a Millennial, Trish, is based on the aggregated data of Millennials I have studied, but the reason I use the name Trish throughout this book is because the "real" Trish is a 29-year-old leader who is perhaps one of the best mentors I have ever studied. She, like all Millennials, appreciates how to shift her conversations on a dime, enabling others to learn. The Millennial motto is "adapt, adopt, and improve." Millennials can rebuild, redesign, and reframe in a relatively short period of time. They are flexible and enjoy either role, mentor or mentee, although Trish told me that she also "loves" being mentored because she feels it helps her thrive.

Gen Zers' Mentoring Motivator

When you need a fresh perspective on interacting with your customers, ask a Gen Zer. If you have a problem and can't solve it, ask a Gen Zer to "have a go at it." Gen Zers are natural learners and soak up information like a sponge. In the few cases I have studied Gen Zers acting as mentors, they have proved themselves skillful at using both global and local examples, thereby adding more texture to the solution. Like Millennials, as young team members, their biggest asset is their global perspective on problem solving.

HOW TO CREATE THE PERFECT MENTORING PROGRAM

Now that you understand how each generation operates best as a mentor, it's time for you to learn how to actually implement a mentoring program in your organization.

Over the years I have helped more than 30 organizations introduce mentoring with my system, called the Donohue Mentoring System (DMS), and the results have been astounding:

- Mentors and mentees who participated in the DMS reported that after completing the program, they felt they were 32 percent more committed to the organization and 46 percent more satisfied with their jobs than their peers who did not participate. They also missed much less work and reported significantly fewer doctor visits, which meant healthcare savings and less lost time for the employees' companies.

- Of all the relationships created during the DMS, 90 percent of them continued to thrive nine months after the program, according to my 2018 data.

- Among participants, 94 percent believed the DMS made them better collaborators.

So how can you make those changes a reality in your organization? By introducing my DMS. Let me show you how.

The Donohue Mentoring System

To create your own program that cultivates partnerships, follow these steps:

Step one: determine the purpose of starting a mentoring program. The purpose should be to increase team member engagement, increase productivity, or stimulate critical thinking between the generations. Mentoring provides context, defines success, and offers opportunities for learning. Often, it consists of building a relationship, creating dialogue, and matching words with deeds. The concept of ethical leadership, designed in the '70s, assumed that people knew how to be mentors and mentees. The DMS does not make the same assumption. The DMS is designed to test you and enable you to increase your mentoring abilities. Good mentoring programs work within the rigor and structure of today's human resource systems and with the time constraints most mentors and mentees face daily.

Step two: determine how you are going to recruit mentors and mentees. You have one of two options:

- **Compulsory mentoring** occurs when mentors and mentees are told they have to participate. With this method, as management, you decide who is selected to be the mentors and the mentees. Most often, your HR or leadership teams have ideas on who should be included. Recruitment in this type of mentoring works best with Gen Xers, who are often the most reluctant to mentor or become a mentee because they worry that time in a mentoring relationship is time away from a task. To motivate this group to participate, use the self-preservation mentoring motivator. For example, explain that by being a mentor in this program, participants will increase their teams' productivity and critical thinking through collaboration.

- **Self-selection mentoring** occurs when the participants fill in an application and opt in to the program. This style of choosing candidates for a mentoring program works best for Millennials and Gen Xers. It meets their confidence and democracy motivator because everyone in the organization has a chance to fill in the application and apply to the program.

Step three: design an application, explain the requirements for the program (including how much time the program will take), and clearly explain who can, and should, apply. Examples of application questions include the following:

1. Are you willing to go the extra mile and prepare for your mentoring?

   Yes

   No

2. You are being asked to commit to mentoring one mentee for 30 minutes a week for 16 weeks. Can you do this with your job?

   Yes

   No

3. A corporate mentor is a resource, helping hand, sounding board, and referral service. The job of a corporate mentor is to provide mentees with support, encouragement, and information. During the DMS, the mentees will be asked to choose three goals that they would like to achieve during the program. These goals will come from their managers or their most recent reviews. Are you comfortable with helping the mentees achieve their goals during this period?

   Yes

   No

4. Typically, we have found that the following challenges impede success for both mentors and mentees in the program:

   - People feel they are too busy to devote time to the program

   - People volunteer for mentoring because they think it will get them a promotion

   - People hold rigid opinions and are resistant to change

   - People want to mentor to work out their personal issues

If you feel that you may currently fall into any of these categories, please opt out of the program and discontinue the application.

Step four: pair mentors and mentees together—ask yourself what makes a good fit for a mentoring collaboration. An example from the DMS program is as follows:

> When we recruit mentors and mentees, we strive to ensure that they fit with the program. The DMS is very structured. It requires discipline and provides mentors and mentees with many valuable learning experiences. Often, we find that people that are too busy to mentor opt out of the program before it begins, which is good, because time management is essential in mentoring. If someone does not have experience in mentoring, that *should not* deter him or her.

Step five: create the program and structure. Table 6.3 shows an example of what we use in the DMS to create the program and structure, but I also recommend reviewing Harvard's ManageMentor service. This table satisfies Gen Xers because it provides and explains what "winning" looks like, but it also serves as a syllabus for Millennials and Gen Zers, providing them with a structured overview of what will be accomplished during the program and enabling everyone to collaborate more effectively.

TABLE 6.3: **Weekly Overview**

Week	Theme	Materials	Objective	Delivery	Participant Requirement
Pre-work	Introduction	Worksheet	Participants are provided with an overview of the program	Meeting or conference call (available online for those who can't call in)	All participants receive survey, via link, to complete
Pre-work	Tools for success	Handbooks and textbook	Matching; students given online learning platform password	Introduction email	Read materials
Week #1	Delivering business results and performance	"Creating the Best Workplace," *HBR*, May 2013	Understanding your goals and our culture	All participants will receive an email enabling them to log in to their agenda and tools for Week #1	First meeting, either by phone or in person (note, all meetings can be changed or merged to accommodate travel and vacations)
Week #2	Joint value and the power of listening in culture	Listening exercise	Listening and joint value	All participants will receive an email enabling them to log in to their agenda and tools for Week #2	Second meeting, either by phone or in person; all participants will receive link to an optional learning journal

Step six: create mentor and mentee assessment sheets. Build your assessment into already existing performance reviews or use Glint, a program that uses daily questions to assess employee performance. Figure 6.1 provides an example of my pre- and post-survey for the DMS. You will notice the exact same series of questions shown twice, but I have included a mentor version and mentee version to reflect the experience of each type of participant.

4. To what degree are you an effective mentee?

	Strongly disagree	Disagree	Somewhat disagree	Unsure	Somewhat agree	Agree	Strongly agree
Good listener	○	○	○	○	○	○	○
Available to my mentor	○	○	○	○	○	○	○
Nonjudgmental	○	○	○	○	○	○	○

4. To what degree are you an effective mentor?

	Strongly disagree	Disagree	Somewhat disagree	Unsure	Somewhat agree	Agree	Strongly agree
Good listener	○	○	○	○	○	○	○
Available to my mentee	○	○	○	○	○	○	○
Nonjudgmental	○	○	○	○	○	○	○

FIGURE 6.1: DMS Pre- and Post-Survey Examples

Step seven: begin!

These seven steps might seem like a lot to implement right now, but if you continue to read, you'll see how easy, and important, it is to establish a mentoring program in your organization, as shown in the real-life story of one of my clients.

DMS in Action

Have you ever felt lost and alone at work, unsure of who to ask for help? Kalvin Hardy did. Kalvin is a college-educated, brilliant young

Millennial who didn't understand what his leader needed and why, and he was unclear on how he was to achieve his goals. He had only been with Walmart for three months, and his manager had not had time to work with him to help him understand the company's workplace culture. Kalvin lacked the structure to collaborate. He was unhappy and wanted to leave, but his bosses recognized him as a valuable asset and didn't want to lose him. They knew his unhappiness was rooted in not understanding how people collaborated among the many different teams at Walmart. They asked him if he would be willing to stay if they could "teach him the ropes."

Mentoring for retention was therefore the purpose of Kalvin's mentoring program. The program aimed to accomplish three goals: one, teach Kalvin how to collaborate within the culture; two, communicate how to cultivate intergenerational partnerships within Walmart; and three, present a framework of problem solving that would keep Kalvin at the company. When thinking about who to pair Kalvin with to accomplish these objectives, the team outlined two key attributes: experience as an hourly employee who had moved to management and a well-networked associate (Walmart's name for a team member).

They needed Mike Camp, who answered the call when Kalvin's boss emailed out a request to her network for someone to mentor Kalvin. Mike, a Gen Xer, self-selected to mentor Kalvin because he knew the benefits of mentoring. Mike is currently a general manager at a Walmart in Arkansas.

Rather than create an application for this mentoring program, Mike created what is now referred to as a WHOA conversation to determine suitability. WHOA stands for work, home, and other areas of interest. Mike created the PowerPoint slide shown in Figure 6.2 and sent it to Kalvin to see if Kalvin would be interested in having him as his mentor.

FIGURE 6.2: WHOA Poster:
Mike Camp, General Manager #9149

Kalvin was definitely interested because he would have the opportunity to learn from someone who had started off as an hourly employee and now held a management role, which was exactly what Kalvin wanted to achieve. Kalvin created his own WHOA slide and sent it off to Mike. The two have remained mentor and mentee since.

Mike and Kalvin are a perfect mentoring match. When I first talked to them to ensure they were committed to the mentor–mentee relationship, they were both already excited about collaborating on Kalvin's career at Walmart by using the structured mentoring DMS format. Kalvin, a typical Millennial, appreciated that Walmart was providing him with a "real" mentoring program, not just asking him to casually chat with people. He also appreciated that he was not a direct report of Mike's and would get a new point of view from him.

Mike, a Gen Xer, appreciated that the program only required 20-minute weekly sessions with Kalvin. He knew he could find time for 20 minutes per week to mentor Kalvin. Mike's only concern when considering being a mentor had been time, as he himself had been moving up the leadership ladder and was a very active father of two.

Mike remembered from a program he ran for Walmart's Leadership Academy that the step-by-step guide the DMS provided would allow for exactly that. So he reached out to me, and together we created a time commitment for his and Kalvin's mentoring sessions, shown in Figure 6.3.

Weeks	Pre	Week #1	Week #2	Week #3	Week #4	Week #5	Week #6	Week #7	Week #8	Week #9	Week #10	Week #11	Week #12	Week #13	Week #14	Week #15	Week #16	Post	Hours
Mentoring Sessions		20 Mins	20 Mins	20 Mins	20 Mins	20 Mins	20 Mins	20 Mins	20 Mins	20 Mins	20 Mins	20 Mins	20 Mins	20 Mins	20 Mins	20 Mins	20 Mins		5 Hours, 20 Minutes
Workshop #1	90 Mins																		90 Minutes
Mentoring Textbook	4 Hrs.																		4 Hours
Con Call			30 Mins																30 Minutes
Workshop #2									90 Mins										90 Minutes
Con Call													30 Mins						30 Minutes
Workshop #3																90 Mins			90 Minutes
Pre-test	20 Mins																		20 Minutes
Post-test																		20 Mins	20 Minutes
																		Total:	15 Hours, 30 Minutes

FIGURE 6.3: Mentoring Certificate of Completion—
Required Actions Chart

Before their first meeting, Kalvin was asked to write up his desired outcomes and participate in benchmarking to ensure that the mentor–mentee relationship would be productive. Kalvin's planned area of development included building confidence in himself and leaders. Once Mike understood Kalvin's goals, he was able to review other aspects of Walmart training that Kalvin would be exposed to and structure conversations that would fill the training gap. (I have presented examples of these conversations at the end of this chapter.)

Once they got started, Kalvin soared within the organization with Mike's mentorship—and he stayed at Walmart as a result. He not only moved from being an hourly employee to management, but to this day he is still more productive because of what he learned from Mike. Today, he recruits new hires at Walmart, and he is far more willing to collaborate. In his own words, Kalvin expressed to me what he has learned from his mentor, Mike:

> I learned that I need to show people what I am capable of doing. Too many people see me as "quiet Kalvin." They don't get to see what I can really offer. I feel like I am truly confident in who I am now. It felt good to leave these meetings with Mike knowing that I presented myself as an intelligent, confident, and ambitious young man that has something to offer. I've learned so much about myself through this program. It's really helped me to develop confidence, which was my first area of opportunity. My other two goals really stem from confidence. Therefore, I have seen drastic improvements in those areas too.
>
> The most important thing I took away from this program is that I am the key factor in my success. I didn't realize how much power and control I have in shaping my future. I am ready to apply for my promotion and will stay at Walmart because of this program.[9]

Mike walked away from this experience a winner too. Mentoring has been proved to benefit not just the mentee but also the mentor. Mike put it best when he explained the following:

> I can influence others by sharing my experiences and my personal learning to help my mentees build their skills, self-confidence, and influence. Sharing with my mentees how to influence others when you are not in a leadership role can help them build their own influence and positively impact their career development. Through mentoring, I can

demonstrate my passion, knowledge, and skills. This will help me grow and further develop my skills as a leader.[10]

HOW TO CREATE YOUR OWN MENTORING PROGRAM

Mike and Kalvin only had a short period of time together each week, so I created mentoring lessons that were short, focused, and customized for Kalvin.

Since my experience with Mike and Kalvin, I have discovered that anything more than five weeks, or once a month for five months, works well for most mentor and mentee partnerships. When you are creating your mentoring program, adapt the follow conversations based on your already existing training or leadership attributes. Doing so will enable you to scale your mentoring program.

A financial institution I consulted for cleverly used the framework of its individual program plans (IDPs) to adapt the mentoring conversations and make them relevant to the organization on a global scale. When you create a structure for mentoring, keep it simple, clear, and easy to follow.

The following four examples of mentor and mentee conversations are focused on global issues that every team member who wants to be a leader will face. I customized them by using a **mentoring conversation arc**, the framework used to resolve a concern or overcome an obstacle and achieve a goal. In order to use a mentoring conversation arc to build your mentoring conversations, follow these four steps to develop a clear understanding of the organization's culture:

1. Understand the communication structure within the culture in which you will be operating (for example, consider how members email one another or whether they use voice mail).

2. Design opportunities for successful collaboration and create a plan for change.

3. Leverage feedback to make improvements to your performance.

4. Put this all together to identify the structure of feedback (for example, will you communicate daily through emails or phone conversations? Do you use 360 career feedback? How are conflicts solved? What is the driving ethos of the organization?).

Please note each conversation that follows takes 20 minutes and is relatively formal. This helps prevent people from telling stories about what "used to be" and helps them focus on what is happening now.

Conversation #1: Culture, Leadership, and Collaboration

This conversation is designed as an introduction to leadership within the organization and so that the mentee will appreciate the organization's culture. The sequence of the conversation, and the person who starts the conversation, is shown:

1. Mentor shares the guiding principles of the organization and how they align with his or her leadership practice. Mentors should feel free to give examples. (Five minutes)

2. Mentor defines the organization's expected code of conduct. For example, how are emails best handled? Or what is the expectation to work on weekends or outside of a shift? (Five minutes)

3. Mentee outlines his or her personal commitment to work. For example, what is the mentee's commitment to his or her team, work, self, and family? (Five minutes)

4. Mentor and mentee share their societal commitments. For example, what will they do to make the world a better place and how will they do it? (Five minutes)

Conversation #2: Listening and Collaborating

This conversation takes culture to the next level and shows the mentee the structure of how members of the organization listen to and learn from each other. The sequence of the conversation, and the person who starts the conversation, is shown:

1. Mentor reviews why listening is critical to collaboration. (Three minutes)

2. Mentor and mentee both take the VAK test (see Chapter 1) and share with each other how they prefer to receive information. (Sixteen minutes)

3. Mentor and mentee both thank each other. (One minute)

Conversation #3: Creating a Road Map for Collaborating Together

This conversation is designed as a teaching tool that enables mentees to "see" what a successful collaboration looks like and to identify how they can plan a successful collaboration within the parameters of the organization. The sequence of the conversation, and the person who starts the conversation, is shown:

1. Mentee creates two columns on a piece of paper, using the headings "Problem" and "Resources." (One minute)

2. With the mentor, the mentee should define and write down his or her goal and its relationship to collaborating and succeeding in the organization. (Two minutes)

3. Using their experience in the organization, the mentor should help the mentee brainstorm in order to define any macro issues he or she might be facing when it comes to achieving his or her goal. For example, in one such conversation, a mentee learned the reason her boss thought she couldn't prioritize: she didn't answer emails right away. Her company had a sunset rule, which meant she had to answer all the emails she received by the end of day. (Two minutes)

4. Using their experience in the organization, the mentor should help the mentee brainstorm in order to define any micro issues he or she might be facing when it comes to achieving his or her goal. For example, in one such conversation, a mentor helped a mentee understand that her academic presentation style wasn't working for senior leaders because they wanted quick hits of information during meetings, followed by in-depth information sent after the meetings. (Two minutes)

5. Based on experience and contacts, the mentor should identify and note the partners and resources that could be used to overcome the roadblocks identified in order for the mentee to achieve success. (Nine minutes)

6. Together, the mentor and mentee should brainstorm solutions and immediate action steps. For example, in one

conversation, one mentor taught her mentee how to apply for the corporate top-talent program. It was an online process on the company's internal website—they filled out the application together. (Four minutes)

Conversation #4: Feedback and Presentations

This conversation enables mentees to learn the value and importance of feedback when presenting to the group they are collaborating with. The sequence of the conversation, and the person who starts the conversation, is shown:

1. Prior to the mentoring session, the mentee should prepare a five-minute presentation of his or her problem and the solution he or she has developed. Remember, in a quick presentation, mentees want the audience to understand the point of their problems and the solutions. Simply put, the mentee should explain the importance of the problem identified and why it is important to solve. Mentees should remember their VAK and include language that their audience will identify with.

2. Mentee shares his or her presentation. (Five minutes)

3. Mentor offers feedback to the mentee by using the following questions, in the following order:

   a. Did the mentee offer proof that resources should be committed to solving the problem? (Four minutes)

   b. Did the mentee demonstrate any challenges the solution presents, including opposition that might surface? (Five minutes)

   c. Did the mentee rebut this opposition? (Three minutes)

4. Finally, the mentor and mentee should discuss how these steps could be used to increase collaboration when presenting a solution. Mentor should feel free to use personal examples. (Three minutes)

Mentoring acts as a stimulant for generations to effectively collaborate. Rather than creating collaboration overload, as we know so many professionals face today, mentoring lightens your workload because you discover how to create efficiencies in collaboration. This leads to higher productivity and mastery, which we will learn about in the next, and final, chapter.

CHAPTER SEVEN

STEP 7:
REALIZE YOUR POWER
AS A COMMUNICATOR

DIGITAL HARMONIZATION

My friend Fredrick shared a very sensible thought with me the other day: "No matter what language you speak, you can always understand the phrase 'please pass the wine.'"

If you have traveled outside your native land and are a language Luddite like me, you know how this phrase rings true. People want to connect with other people. We find a way to make ourselves understood to get what we need. I tend to raise my voice if I am not being understood. Then I resort to hand gestures, such as pretending I have a glass of wine in my hand and lifting it to my lips. If I'm ordering wine in a restaurant and the waiter still doesn't understand me, this usually results in my yelling "wine" and gesturing with my invisible glass. At this point exhaustion sets in, and I need a bottle, not just a glass.

Communicating in the modern workplace is much the same experience. It takes a lot of effort to get your point across—oftentimes too much effort. Communicating through digital technology every day is exhausting, which increases the stress you feel. To lessen your stress, you'll probably step back from what you are doing and disengage from your colleagues or team members. If you are like me, you can only yell and wave your arms for so long.

Each of the previous chapters has presented you with patterns, or generational anchoring benchmarks (GABs), that you can use to identify the stress triggers that prevent the message sent from being the message received. This chapter brings together the threads woven throughout the book and is full of tips to remove those triggers to ensure the message sent *is* the message received. It is what I call **digital harmonization**, the classification of digital social behavior and recognition of digital social cues in messages and meetings.

THE MODEL T OF DIGITAL COMMUNICATION

My great-grandfather was one of Henry Ford's first engineers, and because of that family history, I have always been fascinated with Ford and his automation process. Unofficial family lore (aka Irish gossip) has it that my grandfather once asked Ford why the Model T became so successful. Ford said, "I did something while everyone else waited. Our competitors tried to make something perfect." In this book, I have presented what I like to think of as the Model T of digital communication. It isn't a perfect system, but it will get you where you need to go, which is what the Model T did.

In each chapter, I have given you patterns or social cues about the modern workforce that enable you to harmonize your digital communication (as outlined in Figure 7.1), resulting in clear understanding that reduces fatigue, stress, and lack of productivity. When you begin to use these patterns, you can process information with a new efficiency through technology and with less assumption. Time is saved, stress is reduced, things get done, and more money is made.

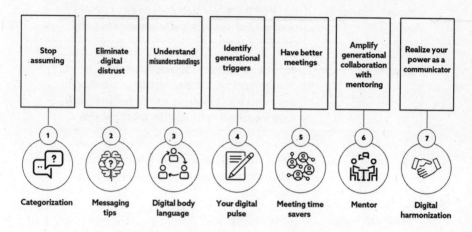

FIGURE 7.1: The 7 Steps to Breaking Down
Communication Barriers at Work

The following is a brief overview of each generation to help you put Figure 7.1 into action.

Boomers Summarized

TABLE 7.1: **Boomers Summarized**

Digital Intelligence Driver	Auditory, Task Default
To avoid assumption	When emailing, follow the rules of grammar and proper phrasing
To avoid digital distrust	Align your message with the mission of the organization; if you do not receive a timely response, call them and encourage a discussion

Digital Intelligence Driver	Auditory, Task Default
Understand misunderstandings	When Boomers receive feedback, they like it to be direct but respectful; they appreciate being asked detailed questions and anticipate, and look forward to, being pressed for answers
Generational triggers	Boomers use consensus building in committees to move a project forward; they will dial into a meeting if they cannot attend in person; email is their technology preference; and they are reluctant to embrace video
How to break down collaboration barriers	Remember that Boomers are honorable leaders who pledge to the mission; don't be afraid of discussing failure with members of this group—they see it as a learning tool
Meeting preference	Status meetings
Tips for digital harmony	The stress trigger for Boomers is not being able to have a dialogue, as dialogue is key to engaging and influencing them to get something done; conversation and debate are the cues and prompts that facilitate Boomers' learning success

Boomers use auditory processing to comprehend information given to them by leaders and teammates. Their schooling, which revolved around debates and language, and their relationship to technology provide the foundation for this preference. Boomers are committed to their leaders, as well as to the mission and the values of the organization. They built a legacy and are concerned about preserving it. They are inspired by conversations that build trust.

Some key tips for good collaboration with Boomers are as follows:

- Accept and give feedback to build trust, and have difficult conversations that result in change.

- A stress trigger for Boomers is having their opinions be ignored—they can't build if no one is listening.

- Cues and prompts that facilitate Boomers' success are presenting a logical process, including all the facts and figures, and providing the background reading.

- The stress trigger that stops Boomers from being their best selves in a team is when someone tells them, "You don't know . . ." Instead, ask them to share their knowledge.

- Cues and prompts that facilitate Boomers' collaboration include asking, "What is your experience?" Their learning preferences are auditory. In a brainstorming session they love to talk things out. Don't be afraid of silence; if Boomers are quiet, they may be thinking of a highly creative solution, so give them time to complete their thoughts.

Gen Xers Summarized

TABLE 7.2: **Gen Xers Summarized**

Digital Intelligence Driver	Visual, Task Default
To avoid assumption	When emailing, ensure the message relates to the goal and the vision of the project or organization
To avoid digital distrust	Align your messages to Gen Xers with the vision of the organization and include social proof in the form of a PowerPoint; give them time to think
Understand misunderstandings	When Gen Xers receive digital feedback, they skim what they are reading—they want to know whether they have achieved the goal, and if they haven't, they will think about how they can turn it around; give them direction to help them succeed

Digital Intelligence Driver	Visual, Task Default
Generational triggers	Gen Xers make decisions based on the objectives of the project, think in terms of gray, and weigh all the options; the question "What if?" plagues them, and they often think about it far too late in the night; a shared drive, such as Google Drive, enables them to go back and see previous editions of a document to create the next version
How to break down collaboration barriers	Remember that Gen Xers are command-and-control leaders who align with the vision of the organization or team; they are great strategists; if you challenge them with "How are we going to do this?" they will take the ball and run with it
Meeting preference	Customer meetings
Tips for digital harmony	When Gen Xers get stressed during a project, they tend to take everything on themselves, as they don't trust others to get it done; cues and prompts that motivate Gen Xers include "we need your vision," "give it a try," and "do it your way"; be straight with them on why a project needs to be done and why they need to do it

Gen Xers visually process information from leaders and teammates. Their schooling and relationship to technology provide the foundation for this preference. Gen X was the first generation whose members were "the last hired and the first fired." Bosses knew work was scarce when Gen Xers began their careers, and some wanted these new members of the workforce to be fearful for their jobs because "competition was the best thing." The winners were promoted, and the losers were fired.

Some key tips for good collaboration with Gen Xers are as follows:

- Accept and give feedback to build trust, and have difficult conversations that result in change.

- Stress triggers for Gen Xers occur when they don't know how to make something work. Give them the "how" before you ask them to "do," and if it is related to new technology, make sure you point out its value to the bottom line.

- Cues and prompts that facilitate Gen Xers are visual ones, particularly PowerPoint decks and presentations. Next best are visual maps, infographics, or charts if you don't want to use PowerPoint to engage.

Millennials Summarized

TABLE 7.3: **Millennials Summarized**

Digital Intelligence Driver	Kinesthetic, Share Default
To avoid assumption	When emailing Millennials, be brief—write a message that would fit on a sticky note
To avoid digital distrust	Engage with Millennials through experience; change your method of assessing rewards from task to time
Understand misunderstandings	This generation doesn't accept feedback if they don't see the reason for the task—they will question it; to avoid this back-and-forth with them, quickly outline the logic and then provide the data
Generational triggers	Millennials use social media to make comparisons and decisions—they were taught to share, and technology assists them in making informed decisions; incorporate social media links, including YouTube, into your creative collaborations with them
How to break down collaboration barriers	Remember that Millennials are democratic leaders who are inspired to collaborate by being asked to be a change agent or a disrupter; they naturally work well with others
Meeting preference	Collaboration meetings

Digital Intelligence Driver	Kinesthetic, Share Default
Tips for digital harmony	Stress triggers include not enabling Millennials to share and get ideas from their friends and limiting the use of GIFs, stickers, fun rewards, and gamification of projects and team members; cues and prompts to empower Millennials include being clear in your direction; they love games and video, so let them use them to learn, share, and develop

Millennials were educated in terms of groups—they think in terms of groups and they react in terms of groups. That's why we have such a strong sharing economy. Their parents constantly pushed them into different activities. They always had mentors, coaches, and opportunities to learn because, to their parents, they were the most important people on the planet—another huge shift from previous generations' parents. In the past, learning was a privilege; Millennials' parents made sure it became a right, and Millennials expect the same from work. Learning from others is, and always will be, a way of life for them.

Millennials have also been the most scheduled generation yet. Growing up, they didn't have playtime, they had play dates. As a result, this generation processes information from leadership in black and white, not gray. Millennials won't trust you unless you walk the walk, not just talk the talk.

Some key tips for good collaboration with Millennials are as follows:

- Accept and give feedback to build trust, and have difficult conversations that result in change.

- Stress triggers for Millennials include such things as a mismatch between your actions and your promises and an effort to buy them with old economy rewards, including money, rather than offering them a clear path for development.

- Cues and prompts for leaders to engage Millennials are simple: give them creative freedom with clear boundaries. Provide black and white directions—not gray.

Gen Zers Summarized

TABLE 7.4: **Gen Zers Summarized**

Digital Intelligence Driver	Visual, Auditory, Share Default
To avoid assumption	When writing emails or texting with Gen Zers, think in very short communication methods such as memes, emojis, and instastories
To avoid digital distrust	This generation has never had to wait for information before, so they don't expect to wait for information from leaders now; provide them with daily feedback *and* the opportunity to give daily feedback in return
Understand misunderstandings	Gen Zers like the comfort of a hierarchy and a clear and consistent path of respectful feedback; they have seen how feedback posted online can derail a conversation
Generational triggers	Use technology to create groups that can share and make decisions but recognize that these groups often lock out people—Gen Zers know how to lock out others who want to "spy" on what they are doing
How to break down collaboration barriers	Remember that Gen Zers are equalitarian collaborators, inspired to collaborate according to ideals and actions that benefit the good of the whole organization; they are very logical in their approach to collaboration
Meeting preference	Collaboration meetings (note, this is a best guess, as data on this cohort are limited)
Tips for digital harmony	Stress triggers for Gen Zers include asking them to learn using only one modality—this generation is creative, using visual and auditory technology and memes; Bing and Google take too long, so they watch videos; cues and prompts include talking "with" them, not "to" them; exercise their social justice DNA for change

Gen Z is the quiet and strong-willed generation, and its members will be the holders of your technology capital. They have grown up with and in the Internet, respectively. The first thing they learned in school was how to go into lockdown when a stranger enters the building. Gen Z is the on-demand generation. Since they grew up with and in technology, Gen Zers have never had to wait. As mentioned, the data on Gen Zers and leadership are thin, as the cohort is just entering the workforce. Research we do have suggests this generation will be hardworking and will value money, much like their Depression-era great-great-grandparents, but they will be transparent about money.

Some key tips for good collaboration with Gen Zers are as follows:

- A fast-emerging stress trigger for Gen Zers is social justice. They won't work for leaders or companies that don't have the same values as they do, which are very global. They don't see the same barriers their grandparents—Boomers—grew up with and around, and they believe in equal work for equal pay.

- Other stress triggers for Gen Zers include using email or answering phones. But because these technologies are not about to be replaced anytime soon, Gen Zers must be taught the basics. Cues and prompts that enable Gen Zers to connect are visual and auditory opportunities to share and learn, for example, memes. Don't plan on them reading.

- Be prepared for this generation to shake up how CEOs and senior leaders are compensated, as this generation will protest and encourage change. Gen Zers have social change built into their DNA, which began with the Occupy movement and its "we are the 99 percent" slogan and hasn't left.

DIGITAL EMOTIONAL INTELLIGENCE (DEQ)

As we learned in the Introduction and Chapter 4, your digital emotional intelligence (DEQ) is your ability to recognize patterns in the messages you receive, enabling you to both *understand* what people are saying to you and *predict* how people are going to engage with you. It empowers you to quickly and effectively solve problems. DEQ also determines if you are **task dominant** or **share dominant**. Table 7.5 shows each generation's task-dominant or share-dominant traits, how to best understand those traits, and how to set the stage for motivating each generation based on those traits.

TABLE 7.5: **Generational Task-Dominant and Share-Dominant Traits**

Boomers	**Task Dominant** Boomers are legacy driven; try to avoid putting them in a nonplace in an open concept office—it tells them that their 30 years of work means nothing
Gen Xers	**Task Dominant** Gen Xers are very visual; take advantage of this to motivate them by giving them a "pretty space," featuring light and air
Millennials	**Share Dominant** Let Millennials have their space; they don't need to be available 24-7, but give them a clear list of tasks to be completed, set meeting times, and introduce consequences and rewards
Gen Zers	**Share Dominant** Gen Zers like to be connected physically and digitally; they will congregate (closely) to look at each other's phones—if you have a chance, watch them as they interact and listen to one another

Eliminate the Barrier of Assumption: The VAK System

Categorization is the brain's shortcut to success when eliminating digital assumption. VAK, as shown in Chapter 1, is a system of categorization that allows you to notice patterns in coworkers' emails, presentations, texts, and even PowerPoints. These patterns are clues as to how your coworkers prefer to communicate and how they prefer you to communicate with them—knowing how to recognize them eliminates assumption. Table 7.6 will help you recognize these patterns.

TABLE 7.6: **Generational Communication Patterns**

Boomers	**Auditory, Task Default** When engaging with Boomers, be direct and grammatically correct
Gen Xers	**Visual, Task Default** When talking with Gen Xers, draw them a picture or show them a visual of what you need them to do; better yet, ask them to design a visual of the project
Millennials	**Kinesthetic, Share Default** With Millennials, ask them what they would do in a given situation and to research and report their findings back to you; ensure that you give them a very clear definition of what you are looking for
Gen Zers	**Kinesthetic, Visual, Share Default** With Gen Zers, share technology and think in short sharp sentences, like with social media; ask them to create a picture of how they feel; then ask them to repeat what you have said to ensure they heard you; follow up by asking them to relate that to what they have seen online or how this has been done in the past and what they would suggest; finally, ask them to set their listening goals and allow them to use technology

Bust the Barrier of Digital Trust: Technology Anchors

Generational anchoring benchmarks around trust are derived from common generational experiences, patterns at school, and early career experiences with technology. Trust anchors help people frame problems, solutions, and encounters by using technology. Trust anchors help you understand why people use technology the way they do. Common technology trust anchors for each generation are shown in Table 7.7.

TABLE 7.7: **Technology Trust Anchors**

Boomers	**Phone Calls** Boomers are very good at taking a direct command from a leader—they don't question the direct command; they look at how this command is going to help them build their organization
Gen Xers	**Individual Technology** Gen Xers take command, put their head down, and get the job done, but they are always wary of the consequences; it is essential to build trust with Gen Xers and work hard to keep it
Millennials	**Social Technology** Millennials go to their social network to double-check what they are hearing to confirm whether it is true; yes, it may be frustrating, but a leader needs to accept it and perhaps even learn from it
Gen Zers	**The Cloud** Gen Zers must be able to keep their smartphones: Instagram, SnapChat, and all the "instant com apps" are very much like what the telephone once was to previous generations—their means of communication

Defeat the Barrier Caused by Digital Feedback: Digital Body Language

Digital body language includes the technology you choose to deliver the message, the words you choose, the order of your words, the rhythm of your writing, and the pace. Appreciating each generation's digital body language enables you to understand and leverage the context of their conversations with you, enabling you to provide them with clear feedback. Table 7.8 gives suggestions on how to provide digital feedback to members of different generations.

TABLE 7.8: **Types of Digital Feedback**

Boomers	**Dignified** Include accomplishments and how listing accomplishments can help others
Gen Xers	**Strong** Show Gen Xers exactly what is happening; use a visual, outline the big picture, and show them where they will encounter particular obstacles
Millennials	**Appealing** Tell Millennials their value; show them how they will be developed and demonstrate a means to an end.
Gen Zers	**Be Helpful and Nice** Think quick engagement; say to them, "This will help you to do your work," and give them time to absorb what you have said; then ask them to tell you what they understood you to have said

Overcome the Barrier in Digital Collaboration: Sentence Patterning

To reduce collaboration-limiting cultural stress in your organization, identify digital collaboration norms to help team members manage up and down. Similar to a protocol for solving an IT or an HR problem, create a collaboration protocol, derived from generational triggers, that engages each generation. Table 7.9 shows each generation's preferred form of collaboration.

TABLE 7.9: **Generational Collaboration Protocols**

Boomers	Prefer an email in the form of a letter (for example, "Dear [insert name],"), and they like well-written correspondence
Gen Xers	Appreciate brevity and PowerPoint decks; when collaborating with Gen Xers, use charts and to-do lists with calendar invitations and follow up with a deck and clear guidelines
Millennials	Like everything to be in black and white; when collaborating with Millennials, send an email invitation, provide an agenda with supporting links, and tell them only what they need to know
Gen Zers	Do not email, so you must teach them; Gen Zers prefer to collaborate with their smartphones in their hands

Conquer the Barrier of Digital Meetings: Meeting Personalities

Meetings are an experience, and this colors how each generation views meetings and meeting technology. By leveraging each generation's preference for meetings (shown in Table 7.10), you can use technology to create and run effective and efficient meetings.

TABLE 7.10: **Generational Meeting Preferences**

Boomers	Prefer military precision
Gen Xers	Prefer relaxed formality

Millennials	Prefer an equal-opportunity environment
Gen Zers	Prefer evenhandedness

Defeat the Barrier of Indifference: Mastery

Indifference is not accepting, nor caring, how each generation processes information through technology. Each generation has an anchor, or bias, for how they like to send and receive digital messages (shown in Table 7.11). Being able to shift technologies to meet the needs of each generation creates the opportunity for clear communication, which according to Warren Buffett, and as mentioned in the Introduction, could increase your net worth by 50 percent.[1]

TABLE 7.11: **Generational Communication Preferences**

Boomers	Phone and talking
Gen Xers	Computer and typing
Millennials	Laptop and sharing of information
Gen Zers	Smartphone and short quick bits of information

THE DOS AND DON'TS FOR "MESSAGE RECEIVED"

Technology is simply a format for people to connect with other people. It is our job as leaders and communicators to humanize technology by being our best authentic selves, which can be accomplished by adapting my version of the Model T system to our personalities and the personalities of those around us.

The Dos

- Every day, apply one lesson learned from the book. None of them are particularly hard.

- Remember the importance of VAK in communicating with each generation.

- Efficiency is effective; each generation is effective through technology in different ways, so learn your GABs.

- Focus on quality, not quantity. Collaborate with team members through generational cues and prompts.

- Run intelligent—not token—meetings and stay on time.

- Keep people happy. To collaborate, meet the communication needs of others and you will reach your goals.

- Make sure others know how you like to communicate. Share the tests in this book with them. Share the GABs. Share the book.

The Don'ts

- Don't respond unless necessary.

- Don't say "Yes" if you don't understand something. Always ask questions.

- Don't speak on behalf of others.

- Don't repeat a negative.

- Don't get too technical. Ask yourself, "Would my mother understand it?"

- Don't use too many acronyms.

- Don't provide a grocery list of information in a PDF or dozens of links.

BEYOND THE WORKPLACE: HELPING OTHERS BENEFIT FROM THIS KNOWLEDGE

At some time in the future, many, if not all, of us will need to have difficult conversations with our parents, siblings, stepsiblings, cousins, and friends about money, death, family, marriage, or managing an overwhelming debt. Although this is a relatively new area of research for me (I began in 2017), I have been developing a system to deploy digital intelligence within families to help reduce the stress and anxiety that our daily digital family life is creating.

I hadn't planned to launch this program until 2022; however, with the advent of the COVID-19 pandemic, I began to test this program with families. Because of the pandemic, families have had to connect via Zoom or FaceTime, having difficult conversations without the benefit of being together to read the usual social cues that come with in-person conversations. Although we *see* people on a Zoom call, we can't really *feel* their presence, see all of their surroundings (and potentially other people in the room), and get a true sense of what they are saying or how they are feeling.

The tools you have learned to use in this book can also help you communicate with your family and friends. The book's principles are ones you can use even if you are in a different country than the people you're communicating with, using apps such as WhatsApp, WeChat, and Microsoft Teams. Family meetings make families work. I learned this from my friend and mentor Tom. To this day, his five siblings, all over 50 years of age, are all living in different parts of the world and still have family meetings just to catch up and avoid feeling isolated and lonely. I hope to eventually write another book on family and digital communication. Check my website, thedigitalwellnesscenter .com, for updates.

After all is said and done, I still believe the most insightful message I learned while researching the material for this book is that people need to connect with other people. Picture yourself at a table with people from four different generations, each understanding one another, each learning from one another, and each basking in the glow of satisfaction that comes from being heard and understood. I believe that communication can take you, as Buzz Lightyear, the Disney hero, famously said, "to infinity and beyond."

Be well and remember, if you need me, I am here.

Dr. Mary

md@thedigitalwellnesscenter.com

NOTES

Introduction

1. Ben Wigert and Sangeeta Agrawal, "Employee Burnout, Part 1: The 5 Main Causes," Gallup.com, July 12, 2018, https://www.gallup.com/workplace/237059/employee -burnout-part-main-causes.aspx.
2. The World Health Organization, "Burn-out: an 'occupational phenomenon,'" International Classification of Diseases, May 28, 2019, https://www.who.int/mental _health/evidence/burn-out/en/.
3. Catherine Clifford, "Billionaire Warren Buffett: This is the 'one easy way' to increase your worth by 'at least' 50 percent," CNBC.com, December 6, 2018, https:// www.cnbc.com/2018/12/05/warren-buffett-how-to-increase-your-worth-by-50 -percent.html.
4. Melinda J. Menzer, "The Great Vowel Shift," Facweb.furman.edu, 2000, http://facweb .furman.edu/~mmenzer/gvs/what.htm.
5. Allan and Barbara Pease, "'The Definitive Book of Body Language,'" *New York Times*, September 24, 2006, https://www.nytimes.com/2006/09/24/books/chapters /0924-1st-peas.html.
6. Wigert and Agrawal, "Employee Burnout, Part 1: The 5 Main Causes."
7. Sheryl Kraft, "Companies are facing an employee burnout crisis," CNBC.com, August 28, 2018, https://www.cnbc.com/2018/08/14/5-ways-workers-can -avoid-employee-burnout.html.
8. Mary E. Donohue and E. Esquivel, "Creativity a Chain Reaction: Understanding the Power of Generational Communication," *Proceedings of the Michigan Academy of Arts, Sciences and Letters*, Mt. Pleasant, Michigan: March 9, 2018 (unpublished).
9. Mary E. Donohue and J. Sheridan, "Collaborative Teams Technology: Increasing ROI in Sales Training," *Proceedings of the Michigan Academy of Arts, Sciences and Letters*, Alma, Michigan: March 1, 2019 (unpublished).
10. The World Health Organization, "Burn-out: an 'occupational phenomenon.'"
11. Jim Harter and Ed O'Boyle, "State of the American Workplace: Employee Engagement Insights for U.S. Business Leaders," Gallup, 2012, https://www.slideshare.net /PingElizabeth/state-of-the-american-workplace-by-gallup.
12. Jim Harter, "Dismal Employee Engagement Is a Sign of Global Mismanagement," Gallup Blog, December 13, 2017, https://www.gallup.com/workplace/231668 /dismal-employee-engagement-sign-global-mismanagement.aspx.

Chapter 1

1. Project Management Institute, "The High Cost of Low Performance: The Essential Role of Communications," PMI.org, May 2013, https://www.pmi.org/-/media/pmi

/documents/public/pdf/learning/thought-leadership/pulse/the-essential-role
-of-communications.pdf.

2. Nicole Branan, "Are Our Brains Wired for Categorization?" *Scientific American*, January 1, 2010, https://www.scientificamerican.com/article/wired-for-categori zation/.

3. Julia Naftulin, "Here's how many times we touch our phones every day," *Business Insider*, July 13, 2016, https://www.businessinsider.com/dscout-research-people -touch-cell-phones-2617-times-a-day-2016-7.

4. Ben Wigert and Sangeeta Agrawal, "Employee Burnout, Part 1: The 5 Main Causes," Gallup.com, July 12, 2018, https://www.gallup.com/workplace/237059/employee -burnout-part-main-causes.aspx.

Chapter 2

1. Christopher W. Hart, "The Power of Unconditional Service Guarantees," *Harvard Business Review*, July 1988, https://hbr.org/1988/07/the-power-of-unconditional -service-guarantees.

2. PayScale, "Most Employees Don't Trust Their Company, Boss or Colleagues," PayScale.com, January 22, 2018, https://www.payscale.com/compensation -today/2018/01/trust-in-workplace.

3. Stephen M. R. Covey and Douglas R. Conant, "The Connection between Em-ployee Trust and Financial Performance," *Harvard Business Review*, July 18, 2016, https://hbr.org/2016/07/the-connection-between-employee-trust-and-financial -performance.

4. Edna Heidbreder, "Special review: Lewin's principles of topological psychology," *Psychological Bulletin*, vol. 34, issue 8, 1937, pp. 584–604, https://psycnet.apa.org /record/2005-11899-002.

5. Joseph T. Mahoney, "The Relevance of Chester I. Barnard's Teachings to Con-temporary Management Education: Communicating the Aesthetics of Manage-ment," *International Journal of Organization Theory and Behavior*, 5, 2002, https:// josephmahoney.web.illinois.edu/Publications/Barnard%202002.pdf.

6. Crowe Associates Ltd., "The Importance of Trust in Teams," crowe-associates.co.uk, accessed May 6, 2020, http://www.crowe-associates.co.uk/teams-and-groups/the -importance-of-trust-in-teams/.

7. Sue Bingham, "If Employees Don't Trust You, It's Up to You to Fix It," *Harvard Busi-ness Review*, January 2, 2017, https://hbr.org/2017/01/if-employees-dont-trust -you-its-up-to-you-to-fix-it.

8. Eugenio Revilla, "Understanding Generational Differences," LinkedIn.com, July 13, 2016, https://www.linkedin.com/pulse/understanding-generational-differences -eugenio-revilla/.

Chapter 3

1. Clifford Nass, *The Man Who Lied to His Laptop: What Machines Teach Us about Human Relationships*, New York: Current, 2012.

2. Alex Ríos, "How badly our brain processes bad feedback . . . and how to do it right," *Medium: Happyforce*, April 2, 2018. https://medium.com/my-happyforce/how -badly-our-brain-processes-bad-feedback-and-how-to-do-it-right-8966fe1ab5f3.

3. Peter Cappelli and Anna Tavis, "The Performance Management Revolution," *Harvard Business Review*, October 2016, https://hbr.org/2016/10/the-performance-management-revolution.

4. Christine Porath, "Give Your Team More-Effective Feedback," *Harvard Business Review*, October 2016, https://hbr.org/2016/10/give-your-team-more-effective-positive-feedback.

5. Kristen Bialik and Richard Fry, "Millennial life: How young adulthood today compares with prior generations," *Pew Research Center: Social & Demographic Trends*, February 14, 2019, https://www.pewsocialtrends.org/essay/millennial-life-how-young-adulthood-today-compares-with-prior-generations.

6. My former professor, Dr. Michael Gilbert, is an expert in distress signs. He learned from Dr. Taibi Kahler's Process Communication Model®. This is my respectful adaptation of their groundbreaking work.

7. Mary E. Donohue, "Administration," *Building Millennials' Loyalty: A Netflix Model*, Western Michigan University, MI: Michigan Academician, 1st ed., vol. XLV, 2017, p. 2.

Chapter 4

1. Jennifer Deal, *Retiring the Generation Gap: How Employees Young & Old Can Find Common Ground*, San Francisco: Jossey-Bass, 2006.

2. Richard Fry, "Millennials are the largest generation in the U.S. labor force," Pew Research Center, April 11, 2018, https://www.pewresearch.org/fact-tank/2018/04/11/millennials-largest-generation-us-labor-force/.

3. Richard Fry, "Millennials are the largest generation in the U.S. labor force,"

4. Richard Fry, "Millennials are the largest generation in the U.S. labor force."

5. Richard Fry, "Millennials are the largest generation in the U.S. labor force."

6. John Hunter, "People Are Part of the Management System," *The W. Edwards Deming Institute Blog*, July 1, 2013, https://blog.deming.org/2013/07/people-are-part-of-the-management-system/.

7. Accel and Qualtrics, *Millennials and Technology at Home*, Issue No. 5 of 10, accessed May 8, 2020, https://www.qualtrics.com/millennials/ebooks/Millennials_And_Tech_At_Home_eBook_All_AK.pdf.

8. Peter Cappelli and Anna Tavis, "The Performance Management Revolution," *Harvard Business Review*, October 2016, https://hbr.org/2016/10/the-performance-management-revolution.

Chapter 5

1. Hanisha Besant, "The Journey of Brainstorming," *Journal of Transformative Innovation*, vol. 2, issue 1, Summer 2016, p. 1.

2. The World Health Organization, "Burn-out: an 'occupational phenomenon,'" International Classification of Diseases, May 28, 2019, https://www.who.int/mental_health/evidence/burn-out/en/.

3. ConStat, *Efficient Meetings*, ConStat private publication, March 2018.

4. Wisconsin Hospital Association, "Why have a meeting?" Wisconsin Hospital Association Quality Center, accessed May 11, 2020, https://www.whaqualitycenter.org/Portals/0/Tools%20to%20Use/Making%20the%20Most%20of%20Meetings/Why%20have%20a%20meeting%20R%202-12.pdf.

5. Edited for grammar.
6. Michael Mankins, Chris Brahm, and Greg Caimi, "Your Scarcest Resource," *Harvard Business Review*, May 2014, https://hbr.org/2014/05/your-scarcest-resource.
7. Martin Luenendonk, "How Much Time Do We Spend in Meetings? (Hint: It's Scary)," *Cleverism*, April 23, 2019, https://www.cleverism.com/time-spent-in-meetings.

Chapter 6

1. Lee Rainie and Janna Anderson, "The Future of Jobs and Jobs Training," Pew Research Center, May 3, 2017, https://www.pewresearch.org/internet/2017/05/03/the-future-of-jobs-and-jobs-training/.
2. Deloitte, "Cracking the code: How CIOs are redefining mentorship to advance diversity and inclusion," Deloitte.com, https://www2.deloitte.com/be/en/pages/technology/articles/cracking-the-code_redefining-mentorship-sponsorship-diversity-inclusion.html.
3. Helene G. Lollis, "Making It Personal: The Four Pillars of High-Impact Mentoring," *Training Industry*, accessed June 8, 2020, https://trainingindustry.com/magazine/issue/making-it-personal-the-four-pillars-of-high-impact-mentoring/.
4. Douglas A. Luke, Ana A. Baumann, Bobbi J. Carothers, et al., "Forging a link between mentoring and collaboration: a new training model for implementation science." Implementation Science, 11, 2016, p. 137, https://doi.org/10.1186/s13012-016-0499-y.
5. Michael Mankins, "Great Companies Obsess Over Productivity, Not Efficiency," *Harvard Business Review*, March 1, 2017, https://hbr.org/2017/03/great-companies-obsess-over-productivity-not-efficiency.
6. Mary E. Donohue (2016). The Death of High Performance Programs: Transferring Knowledge in the New Millennial," *Journal of Diversity Management*, 11 (1), 2016, pp. 1–6, https://doi.org/10.19030/jdm.v11i1.9687.
7. Harvard Professional Development, "Forget Work Perks: Millennial Employees Value Engagement," *Harvard Professional Development Blog*, accessed June 8, 2020, https://blog.dce.harvard.edu/professional-development/forget-work-perks-millennial-employees-value-engagement.
8. Mary E. Donohue, Lorinda Nepaul, Fran McDonald, Pooya Faez, and Chantel Buscema, "Introducing Students to Change in an Unstructured Economy," presentation at the Marketing Management Association Conference, New Orleans, September 2013.
9. Mary Donohue, "The Donohue Mentoring System," *Diversity MBA* magazine, Summer 2013, "Top 100 under 50" issue, edited extract.
10. Mary Donohue, "The Donohue Mentoring System," *Diversity MBA* magazine.

Chapter 7

1. Catherine Clifford, "Billionaire Warren Buffett: This is the 'one easy way' to increase your worth by 'at least' 50 percent," CNBC.com, December 6, 2018, https://www.cnbc.com/2018/12/05/warren-buffett-how-to-increase-your-worth-by-50-percent.html.

GLOSSARY

assumption rate: How often we accept something as certain without evidence to prove its validity. (Introduction)

chronic anxiousness: An exhausted but wired feeling in the body. (Introduction)

collaboration default: How each group prefers to engage in co-operative activities, or your default in how you use technology to get the job done as part of a team. (Introduction)

collaboration motivators: The triggers that stimulate collaboration and break down barriers. (Chapter 6)

compulsory mentoring: Method in which mentors and mentees are told they have to participate. As management, you decide who is selected to be the mentors and the mentees. (Chapter 6)

culture: A set of norms or habits that define a group and enable it to thrive. (Chapter 4)

digital body language: The message you communicate digitally but not through your words. (Chapter 3)

digital emotional intelligence (DEQ): Your ability to recognize patterns in the messages you receive, enabling you to understand what people are saying to you and predict how people are going to engage with you. (Introduction, Chapter 4)

digital harmonization: The classification of digital social behavior and recognition of digital social cues in messages and meetings. (Chapter 7)

digital learning defaults: Your preferences in how you consume information at work and use your communication skills through technology to get the job done. (Introduction)

digital mirroring: The practice of giving information to people in the same manner they provide it to you and others. (Chapter 1)

digital social cues: Patterns in emails, texts, and social media that help people understand the context of the message being communicated. (Introduction)

digital static: The gap between what you write in a digital message and what the person receiving the message understands. (Introduction)

generational anchoring benchmarks (GABs): Cues that will help you understand and categorize messages. Each of the GABs reflects how the economy, technology, leadership trends, and teaching trends have impacted each generation and how these impacts affect each generation's use of technology at work. (Chapter 1)

learning defaults: Mammalian anchoring cues that include how people work, see, hear, and collaborate, which are motivated through your learned social cues. (Introduction)

mentoring circles: Mentoring relationship involving two or more mentees and one mentor. Together, as one unit, the group meets virtually or in person. (Chapter 6)

mentoring conversation arc: the framework used to resolve a concern or overcome an obstacle and achieve a goal. (Chapter 6)

one-on-one mentoring: The traditional form of mentoring, with only one mentee and one mentor involved in the relationship. (Chapter 6)

organizational drag: The structures and processes that prevent people from getting things done. (Chapter 6)

self-selection mentoring: When participants fill in an application and opt in to a mentoring program. (Chapter 6)

share-default learning: Usually applied to Millennials and Gen Zers, representing their introduction to technology as a tool for sharing information. (Introduction)

social cues: Patterns of behavior—such as tone, body language, posture, and familiar gestures—that allow us to reduce the ambiguity in conversation. Social cues allow our brains to accurately predict the meaning of words and can cause a fight-or-flight response to a trigger. (Introduction)

task-default learning: Usually applied to Boomers and Gen Xers, representing their propensity to use technology to complete a task. (Introduction)

teaming: Coming together as a team to achieve a goal. (Chapter 1)

triangle of digital trust: A reference to help you build trust in messaging. Begin by identifying generational trust anchors. Next, utilize the generational frame of reference, and then engage and send your message. In this process, trust is built. (Chapter 2)

workplace culture: How the group acts as a collective to accomplish its goals. (Chapter 4)

INDEX

ABOUT THE AUTHOR

 **Dr. Mary Donohue** has a sincere passion for living and celebrating life. To a large degree, this sincerity is based in her fight to overcome chronic leukemia. The stress of surviving cancer led her to found The Digital Wellness Center. This virtual clinic was designed to reduce stress for all, specifically the stress we experience daily through digital communication.

A social scientist with a focus on digital wellness, Dr. Mary has conducted research and coaching that has benefited companies such as Microsoft, Walmart, American Airlines, TD Bank, Bank of Montreal, OLG, and Kaiser Permanente.

Her work has appeared in *Harvard Business Review*, as research for stories on major networks, in columns for the *Huffington Post* and *Financial Post*, and on-air for all the major news networks.

Recognized by premiers, prime ministers, Queen Elizabeth II, and her peers, Dr. Mary has been honored as one of the "18 Outstanding Women in Tech" and named one of the "Top 100 Women of Influence in America."

Dr. Mary is a yogi, runner, mom, and overall nerd, but for a brief shining moment she will never forget, she was a Supreme (sort of) with Miss Diana Ross.